Response of Ponderosa Pine Stands to Pre-Commercial Thinning

on Nez Perce and Spokane Tribal Forests in the Inland Northwest, USA

Dennis E. Ferguson, John C. Byrne,
William R. Wykoff, Brian Kummet, and Ted Hensold

I0450430

United States Department of Agriculture / Forest Service

Rocky Mountain Research Station

Research Paper RMRS-RP-88

June 2011

Abstract

Stands of dense, natural ponderosa pine (*Pinus ponderosa* var. *ponderosa*) regeneration were operationally, pre-commercially thinned at seven sites—four on Nez Perce Tribal lands in northern Idaho and three on Spokane Tribal lands in eastern Washington. Five spacing treatments were studied—control (no thinning), 5x5 ft, 7x7 ft, 10x10 ft, and 14x14 ft. Sample trees were measured pre- and post-thinning, 3 yrs after thinning, and 5 yrs after thinning, starting in 1997 (Nez Perce sites) and 1998 (Spokane sites). Models of diameter and height growth, change in crown ratio and height to crown base, and probability of western pine shoot borer (*Eucosma sonomana* Kearfott) infestation were developed. Little mortality occurred after thinning, and the trees that died had small crowns. Diameter growth for all of the spacings was significantly different, with widely spaced trees growing faster than narrowly spaced trees. Trees with larger initial diameters or crown ratios had faster post-thinning diameter growth. Spacing had no influence on height growth. Height growth increased with increasing initial tree size, larger crown ratios, and increasing pre-thinning height growth, but decreased with increasing post-thin basal area. Height/diameter ratios (an indication of tree slenderness and stability) increased over time on the narrower spacings, indicating trees were still crowded. We found that thinnings of at least 10x10 ft are needed to stimulate a change in height/diameter ratio. Wider spacings (10x10 ft and 14x14 ft) resulted in lengthening crowns because height to crown base remained closer to the ground, which had implications for fire management. Shoot borer damage occurred on about one-fourth of the sample trees and was negatively correlated with elevation and positively correlated with tree vigor. There was no dramatic non-tree vegetation response to the thinnings, which may be related to herbivory or the lack of ground disturbance from the thinning operations.

Keywords: *Pinus ponderosa*, height growth, diameter growth, height/diameter ratios, thinning from below, crown ratios, competing vegetation

Authors

Dennis E. Ferguson, Research Silviculturist (retired), USDA Forest Service, Rocky Mountain Research Station, Moscow, Idaho.

John C. Byrne, Forester, USDA Forest Service, Rocky Mountain Research Station, Moscow, Idaho.

William R. Wykoff, Research Forester (retired), USDA Forest Service, Rocky Mountain Research Station, Moscow, Idaho.

Brian Kummet, Fee Lands Forester, Nez Perce Tribe, Lapwai, Idaho.

Ted Hensold, Forester (retired), Bureau of Indian Affairs, Spokane Agency, Wellpinit, Washington.

Contents

Acknowledgments

We thank the following for their assistance with this study:

- Nez Perce and Spokane Tribal Executive Committees for access to the study sites;
- John DeGroot, Nez Perce Forestry Director, for his support and direction;
- Melinda Moeur for her help with study design and installation;
- the tribal forestry technicians that implemented the thinning regimes on their respective areas, especially Larry Geffre on the Nez Perce sites, and George Hill, Chuck Kieffer, Marty Andrews, and Harvey Flett on the Spokane sites;
- those who helped with measurements, including Anna McClintick, Laurie Clark-Blackmore, Ben Poulter, Ryan Fogelberg, Marcus Warwell, Dave Hamilton, Kate Schneider, Carson Sprenger, and Marc Antonietti;
- Jerry Rehfeldt for generating spline climate predictions for the seven study sites; and
- Stephen Fitzgerald and David Affleck for reviewing earlier drafts of this manuscript.

Response of Ponderosa Pine Stands to Pre-Commercial Thinning on Nez Perce and Spokane Tribal Forests in the Inland Northwest, USA

Dennis E. Ferguson, John C. Byrne, William R. Wykoff, Brian Kummet, and Ted Hensold

Introction

Ponderosa pine (*Pinus ponderosa*) is one of the most widely distributed conifers in western North America (Oliver and Ryker 1990). Ponderosa pine forests provide tangible and intangible goods and services such as timber, water, wildlife habitat, forage, carbon sequestration, recreation, biodiversity, and aesthetics. In the Inland Northwest, ponderosa pine (*Pinus ponderosa* var. *ponderosa*) grows in a wide variety of conditions, ranging from very dry forests where it is the only conifer species to moist forests where it grows with up to nine other conifer species (Pfister and others 1977; Williams and others 1995; Rehfeldt and others 2008).

Genetic variation of ponderosa pine in the Inland Northwest occurs along relatively steep elevational clines, but with gentle clines for changes in latitude and longitude (Rehfeldt 1991). Growth decreases with increasing elevation, and populations separated by about 1300 ft in elevation tend to be genetically different—that is, they are adapted to different portions of the environmental gradient.

Ponderosa pine often regenerates prolifically, which results in dense stands. Several studies of the effects of thinning naturally regenerated ponderosa pine regeneration have been conducted (e.g., Van Deusen 1968; Barrett 1982; Ronco and others 1985; Cochran and Barrett 1999). These studies have quantified the tradeoffs between greater individual tree growth at lower stand densities versus greater volume production at higher stand densities.

In the Inland Northwest, there is insufficient information on response of ponderosa pine regeneration to thinning. In addition to the question of tree size versus stand volume, tradeoffs of various thinning levels include snow damage, economics, crown dynamics that relate to wood quality, and development of non-conifer understory vegetation. Growth data for ponderosa pine regeneration are especially lacking for our driest ponderosa pine sites. Such data can be used to calibrate ponderosa pine growth in the Forest Vegetation Simulator (FVS, Wykoff and others 1982; Crookston and Dixon 2005). In addition, data from thinning trials can be used to improve prediction of height/diameter ratios in FVS, which are poorly represented (Wonn and O'Hara 2001).

The Nez Perce and Spokane Tribes own and manage ponderosa pine stands that occur on the dry end of the distribution for ponderosa pine in the Inland Northwest. Dense regeneration often occurs as even-aged patches following harvesting or in abandoned fields. The Tribes have multiple objectives for these dry sites, yet data on response to thinning are lacking. The objective of this study was to gather the basic data for evaluating tradeoffs among different post-thin densities on Nez Perce and Spokane Tribal lands.

Methods

This study was established on seven sites—four on Nez Perce Tribal and three on Spokane Tribal lands (Table 1). Initially, a fourth site was installed on the Spokane Tribal lands, but it was burned by a wildfire shortly after thinning. Each site was an area of dense, natural ponderosa pine regeneration in need of pre-commercial thinning. Data were gathered at each site for elevation, slope, aspect, and habitat type (Cooper and others 1991).

Five 250x50 ft experimental units were located at each site to create the greatest uniformity of initial conditions. The long axes of units were oriented parallel with stand or environmental conditions, such as gradients from taller trees to shorter trees, higher to lower topography, or higher to lower seedling density. Because large, uniform contiguous areas of regeneration were not available, installing buffer strips between units was not possible.

One of five treatments was randomly assigned to each experimental unit—control (no thinning), 5x5 ft spacing (~1740 trees/acre), 7x7 ft (~890 trees/acre), 10x10 ft (~435 trees/acre), and 14x14 ft (~220 trees/acre). Ten 1/400-acre circular plots (radius 5.9 ft) were evenly spaced at 45-ft intervals along two lines that transected the long axis of the unit (Figure 1). Each transect was 17 ft from the edge of the unit, and plots were offset within units by starting from opposite ends of the unit. With this plot arrangement, an area about 11 ft wide existed between the edge of the circular plot and the closest boundary between units, which was deemed suitable for studying regeneration-size trees for 5 yrs after thinning. All units had competition at the edges because units did not border non-forested areas. Reukema and Smith (1987) noted no differences in growth rates between interior versus edge trees in plantations that had competition at the edges.

Each increment in spacing from 5x5, 7x7, 10x10, to 14x14 ft doubled the area available for tree growth. We felt a progression of spacings would help evaluate interactions among mortality, lean, crown development, and diameter and height growth.

Table 1. Description of the seven study sites.

Tribe	Name	Elevation (ft)	Slope (%)	Aspect (°)	Habitat type[1]	Pre-thin density (trees/acre)	Latitude Longitude
Nez Perce	Cold Springs	3430	9	150	PSME/SYAL	8280	46.3161 116.4218
Nez Perce	Reubens	3490	15	355	PSME/SYAL	2469	46.3553 116.5585
Nez Perce	West Talmaks	4310	10	60	PIPO/SYAL	9807	46.1597 116.5733
Nez Perce	North Talmaks	4330	16	80	PSME/SYAL	7244	46.1642 116.5663
Spokane	South Castle Rock	1700	0	Flat	PIPO/SYAL	4840	47.9354 118.3349
Spokane	East Castle Rock	1840	18	270	PIPO/SYAL	10,128	47.9404 118.3307
Spokane	Mosquito Heights	2540	11	60	PSME/PHMA	3140	47.9866 118.1819

[1] PSME/SYAL = *Pseudotsuga menziesii/Symphoricarpos albus*
PIPO/SYAL = *Pinus ponderosa/Symphoricarpos albus*
PSME/PHMA = *Pseudotsuga menziesii/Physocarpus malvaceus*

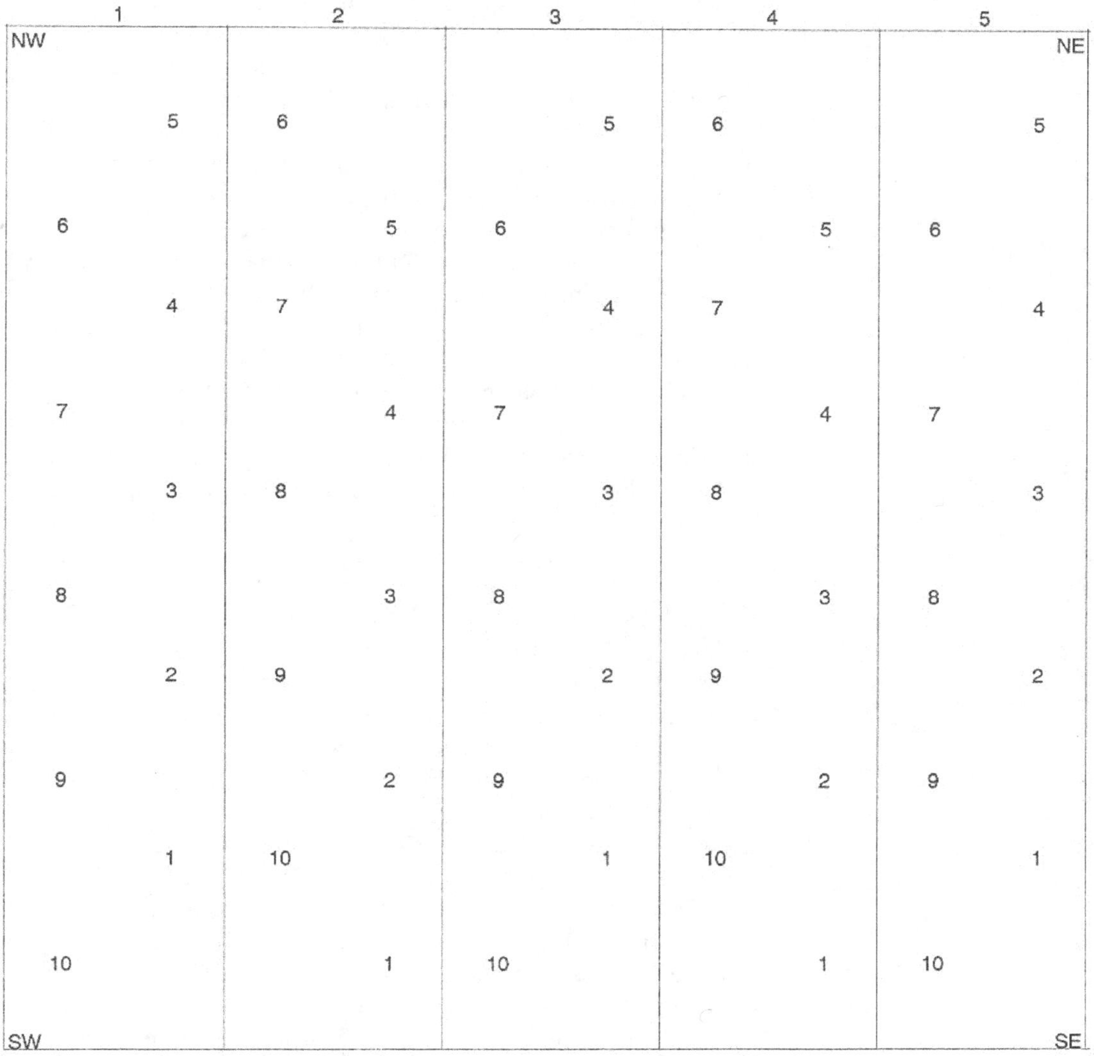

Figure 1. Example plot layout showing 5 experimental units and 10 plots per site.

Pre-thinning measurements were taken at the Nez Perce sites in 1997 and at the Spokane sites in 1998 after the cessation of height and diameter growth. At each 1/400-acre circular plot, height, diameter at breast height (dbh), and species of all trees were measured and recorded. Heavily stocked plots were subsampled using quarter plots as the sampling unit. The quarter plots were delineated using a perpendicular sampling frame. For the first quarter plot, the frame was located with the vertex at plot center so that one leg pointed at, and was perpendicular to, the nearest plot boundary. The other leg was parallel to the boundary and was aimed toward the next plot in the sequence (i.e., for plot 1, the frame was aimed at plot 2). If fewer than 15 trees were found in the first quarter, the frame was moved one quarter in the clockwise direction until a total of 15 trees was obtained. Once any quarter was started, all of the trees in that quarter were measured. The quarters that were measured had to be representative of the plot as a whole in terms of density and tree size; otherwise the whole plot was measured.

Trees sampled on the quarter plots were weighted inversely to the number of quarters sampled to calculate density statistics.

Sites were operationally thinned from below under the direction of Tribal foresters in the fall of 1997 (Nez Perce) and 1998 (Spokane). Thinned trees were left where they fell, except for a few plots at the West Talmaks site, where the thinning was delayed until the spring of 1998 and trees were removed to eliminate the possibility of an outbreak of pine engraver beetle (*Ips pini*) (Livingston 1979).

The first post-thinning measurements were taken in the fall immediately after thinning or in the next spring before trees initiated growth. Density measurements were determined by measuring trees on the 1/400-acre circular fixed-area plot and a concentric variable radius plot (10 ft²/acre basal area factor). Trees less than or equal to 2.3 inch dbh and greater than 1 ft in height were sampled with the fixed-area plot; trees greater than 2.3 inch dbh were sampled with the variable radius plot to quantify competition from trees surrounding the 1/400-acre plot. Basal area/acre and trees/acre were calculated at each plot location based on the measured dbh using standard expansion formulas for each plot type (Avery and Burkhart 1983) and then were summed. If a fixed-area plot was subsampled, then the fixed-area plot density measures were appropriately weighted. Calculated densities from the 10 plots in each treatment were averaged to obtain treatment-level measurements.

Three sample trees were located using the center of each 1/400-acre plot. Sample points were located at the following positions relative to plot center: 1 ft at 60°; 3 ft at 180°; and 5 ft at 300°. Sample trees were the nearest tree to the sample point in each 120° sector, which meant that the sample tree could be outside the 1/400-acre plot. All sample trees were numbered and tagged. Trees were measured at the time of thinning and at 1, 3, and 5 yrs after thinning, following completion of growth for that year. The purpose of measurements at yr 1 and 3 was to detect early responses to thinning, such as mortality, severe lean, physiological shock, or insect problems.

Initially, sample trees in the controls were selected by different rules in the Nez Perce and Spokane sites. At the Nez Perce sites, the three sample trees per plot were chosen by adhering to the rule of the closest tree to the sample points. This sampling rule often resulted in sample trees that would not have been a leave tree in an operational thinning, thus biasing the sample toward small or slender trees. We corrected this bias in the Spokane sites by selecting the closest tree to the sample points that would be a leave tree if the area was to be thinned. During the yr 5 measurement at the Nez Perce sites, we corrected the earlier bias by rating each tree in the control to determine if it would have been a leave tree in an operational thinning. Those trees that would have been a leave tree were used in the analyses, which resulted in the elimination of about one-third of the control trees from the Nez Perce sites. Therefore, sample trees in the control at both locations are comparable.

For each tagged tree, dbh was measured with a tape or caliper to the nearest 0.1 inch. Heights of trees up to 40 ft tall were measured with a telescoping height pole, and a few of the tallest trees were measured using a clinometer. Height was measured to the top of the terminal bud to the nearest 0.1 ft. In order to maximize consistency between sequential measurements on the same tree, all height measurements used the breast height tag as a reference point for 4.5 ft. Height increment for the 5 yrs prior to thinning was determined by measuring height five whorls below the tree top. A subjective ocular estimate of crown ratio was made to the nearest 10 percent. Height to the crown base was measured from the uphill side of the tree to the lowest whorl such that the crown was continuous down to that whorl and at least two branches in the whorl were alive. Tree damages were recorded in marginal notes.

Even-numbered plots were used to record non-tree vegetation and ponderosa pine thinning slash in order to relate thinnings to species occurrence, coverage, and size. A species occurred on a plot if any aerial part of the plant was present within the cylinder defined by a vertical projection of the 1/400-acre plot boundary. These measurements were made 1, 3, and 5 yrs after thinning when vegetation was fully developed (July and August). Depending on species, both the line intercept and canopy coverage methods were used (Canfield 1941; Daubenmire 1959; Chambers and Brown 1983). For the line intercept method, a random azimuth was chosen for each plot, and the transect was laid out to run through the plot center. The transect was divided at the plot center into two radii for recording the length of the radii covered by grasses, forbs, and ponderosa pine thinning slash. The number of forb species per radii was recorded; individual forb species were also recorded, but length of individual forbs along the radii was not recorded. The randomly chosen azimuth for line transects remained the same through subsequent measurements.

A modification of Daubenmire's (1959) canopy coverage method was used to record shrub species. For each shrub species on the 1/400-acre plot, percent cover (ocular estimate) and measured average height were recorded. A value of 1% was used to note occurrence only; otherwise, percent cover classes were 5, 10, 20, 25, 30, 40, 50, 60, 70, 75, 80, 90, 95, and 100%.

Data Analysis

Data were analyzed using methods for mixed models in SAS 9.2 using PROC MIXED (Littell and others 1996). Event data (tree mortality and shoot borer occurrence) were analyzed with PROC GLIMMIX using a dichotomously distributed dependent variable (1 if the event occurs, 0 otherwise). The predicted probability is continuous and bounded in the interval [0,1].

Tree data were analyzed for diameter and height growth, height/diameter (H/D) ratios, height to crown base, and crown ratio change.

Data for shrubs, forbs, and ponderosa pine thinning slash were analyzed for occurrence and percent cover, and height for shrubs. These three variables show if species are expanding by becoming established on more plots (occurrence), expanding horizontally (cover), or expanding vertically (height). Conversely, species could decrease in occurrence, cover, or height.

For all analyses, the statistical significance of independent variables was assessed at the $P = 0.05$ level. LSMEANS was used to detect statistical differences between means. The SUBJECT statement was used to account for the correlation among trees on the same plots; SAS then accounted for these correlations to construct the appropriate test statistics. Transformations of variables were explored to achieve homogeneity of error variance and normality, and to obtain additivity of effects (Kirk 1982). The seven study sites were used as a random variable because results of these analyses should be applicable to similar sites in the Inland Northwest. The significance of independent variables was evaluated using t-ratios and F-values. Akaike's information criteria (AIC, smaller is better), as output by SAS, was used to compare alternative equations that had different independent variables but the same dependent variable. Graphs were prepared to visually inspect whether residuals were centered about the 0 line, with no abnormalities.

Results

Post-Thinning Densities

The data for this study came from naturally regenerated, operationally thinned ponderosa pine stands and should show what can be expected under actual silvicultural prescriptions. Leave trees were not pre-selected. Crews were instructed to thin to the approximate spacing, leaving the best tree in the vicinity specified by the spacing, but with no expectation of rigid spacing. Thus, some variation in spacing did occur.

Table 2 shows mean post-thin spacing by study site. Mean spacings are 3.1 ft between trees in the control, 5.8 ft in the 5x5 ft spacing, 7.4 ft in the 7x7 spacing, 9.4 ft in the 10x10 spacing, and 13.5 ft in the 14x14 spacing. All of the 5x5 spacings exceeded 5 ft between trees, and trees in the Mosquito Heights control averaged 5.1 ft between trees. Even though the spacings were not exact, crews did a reasonable job of creating conditions needed for this study.

Table 2. Mean post-thin ponderosa pine spacing (ft).

Site	Spacing				
	Control	**5x5**	**7x7**	**10x10**	**14x14**
Cold Springs	2.1	5.7	7.7	8.6	13.2
Reubens	4.6	5.9	8.0	10.1	12.0
West Talmaks	2.3	5.7	7.0	9.1	13.1
North Talmaks	1.8	6.7	8.2	11.3	16.3
South Castle Rock	3.9	5.3	7.2	8.8	11.6
East Castle Rock	1.8	5.1	6.4	8.7	15.6
Mosquito Heights	5.1	6.3	7.4	9.0	12.8
Spacing mean	**3.1**	**5.8**	**7.4**	**9.4**	**13.5**

Trees

A total of 973 trees were available for analyses. Five trees were not ponderosa pine, so they were eliminated from analyses. One tree was much larger than other trees (10.5 inches dbh at the beginning of the study) and was eliminated as an outlier. Twenty-three trees killed by a wildfire on a few plots at East Castle Rock in 2001 were also eliminated from analyses. Fifteen trees developed severe lean after thinning and were considered unable to recover and grow vertically. Six of these 15 trees subsequently died. An additional 24 trees died from other causes during the study period. Data summaries for the 905 live trees are given in Table 3, and Table 4 shows average post-thin height (H_0), dbh (D_0), and crown ratio (CR_0) by spacing.

Severe lean

Of the 15 trees that developed severe lean, none occurred in the control. Severe lean trees were mid-size trees, always between heights of 10 and 24 ft, with high H_0/D_0 ratios (slender trees) between 60 and 130. An important finding is that only 1.6% of the sample trees fell over following thinning. Severe lean was first observed at yr 1 for about one-third of the 15 trees, and at yr 3 for the other two-thirds of these trees. Six of the 15 trees died by yr 5 and are discussed in the following section on mortality.

Mortality

Thirty trees (3.1%) died during the 5-yr study. PROC GLIMMIX models (not shown) determined that trees with smaller crown ratios (CR_0); slower 5-yr, pre-thin height growth ($H-5_{grow}$); and higher H_0/D_0 ratios had a higher probability of mortality. Figure 2 is a frequency distribution of crown ratios at the beginning of the study by live/dead status at yr 5. This figure shows that (1) few trees died, and (2) most of the dead trees had small crown ratios. Of the 30 trees that died, 4 were dead at yr 1, 11 more died by yr 3, and 15 more died by yr 5. Mortality was attributed to a wide variety of causes, including pine engraver beetles, animal damage, poor health, severe lean, mechanical damage, and unknown. Thinning stands in the fall of the year allowed slash to dry and avoided a buildup of pine engraver beetle populations.

Table 3. List of variables used in analysis of data and their means and extreme values.

Abbreviation	Explanation	Mean	Min/Max
	Tree variables (unless otherwise noted, N = 905 trees)		
CL_0	Crown length at the time of thinning (H_0-HCB_0). (ft)	9.66	0.3 to 23.8
CL_0/H-5_{grow}	Ratio of crown length to 5-yr height increment prior to thinning. 904 trees.	1.41	0.3 to 3.6
CR_0	Ocular crown ratio the year of thinning.	0.58	0.2 to 0.9
CR_5	Ocular crown ratio at yr 5. 902 trees.	0.60	0.2 to 0.9
CR_{HCB}	Crown ratio calculated using height to crown base.	0.68	0.23 to 0.96
CR_Δ	5-yr change in CR_{HCB}. 900 trees.	-0.035	-0.46 to 0.32
D_0	Diameter at breast height the year of thinning. (inches)	2.75	0.0 to 7.9
D_5	Diameter at breast height at yr 5. 903 trees. (inches)	3.97	0.0 to 10.3
D_{grow}	5-yr diameter increment (D_5-D_0). 868 trees. (inches)	1.21	0.0 to 3.2
H_0	Tree height the year of thinning. (ft)	14.47	1.0 to 36.5
H_5	Tree height at yr 5. 900 trees. (ft)	19.46	2.0 to 43.3
H_0/D_0	Height/Diameter ratio the year of thinning, in identical units ($H_0/[D_0/12.0]$). 867 trees.	67.04	34.7 to 184.0
H_5/D_5	Height/Diameter ratio at yr 5. 892 trees.	62.72	34.4 to 180.0
H_{grow}	5-yr post-thin height increment (H_5-H_0). 900 trees. (ft)	5.0	0.3 to 9.7
H-5_{grow}	5-yr pre-thin height increment. 904 trees. (ft)	6.9	0.8 to 14.7
HCB_0	Height to crown base the year of thinning. (ft)	4.8	0.5 to 16.3
HCB_5	Height to crown base at yr 5. 901 trees. (ft)	7.0	1.0 to 21.0
HCB_Δ	Change in height to crown base (HCB_5 - HCB_0). 901 trees. (ft)	2.2	0.0 to 9.1
	Plot variables (N = 350)		
BA_p	Post-thin plot basal area. (ft²/acre)	41.3	0 to 224
SLO	Plot slope. (%)	11.3	0 to 22
TPA_p	Post-thin plot density (trees per acre)	2048	0 to 37,260
	Experimental unit variables (N = 35)		
BA_0	Pre-thin treatment basal area. (ft²/acre)	78.8	26.7 to 149.0
BA_t	Post-thin treatment basal area. (ft²/acre)	41.3	5.5 to 140.9
SPAC	Class variable for nominal spacings of none (control), 5x5 ft, 7x7 ft, 10x10 ft, and 14x14 ft.	n/a	n/a
TPA_t	Post-thin treatment density. (trees per acre)	2048	164 to 13,997
	Site variables (N = 7)		
E	Elevation. (ft)	3091	1700 to 4330

Table 4. Post-thin means for sample trees by spacing (ft). Within columns, means that are followed by the same letter are not statistically different at the $P = 0.05$ level.

Spacing	H_0 (ft) Mean	H_0 (ft) Std. Dev.	D_0 (inches) Mean	D_0 (inches) Std. Dev.	CR_0 Mean	CR_0 Std. Dev.	N
Control	14.7[a]	7.5	2.77[ab]	1.63	0.59[ab]	0.16	126
5x5	13.5[a]	7.5	2.34[a]	1.48	0.55[b]	0.14	190
7x7	14.2[a]	6.9	2.67[ab]	1.53	0.58[b]	0.14	189
10x10	14.7[a]	6.0	2.83[bc]	1.33	0.57[b]	0.15	201
14x14	15.2[a]	6.0	3.13[c]	1.54	0.62[a]	0.16	199

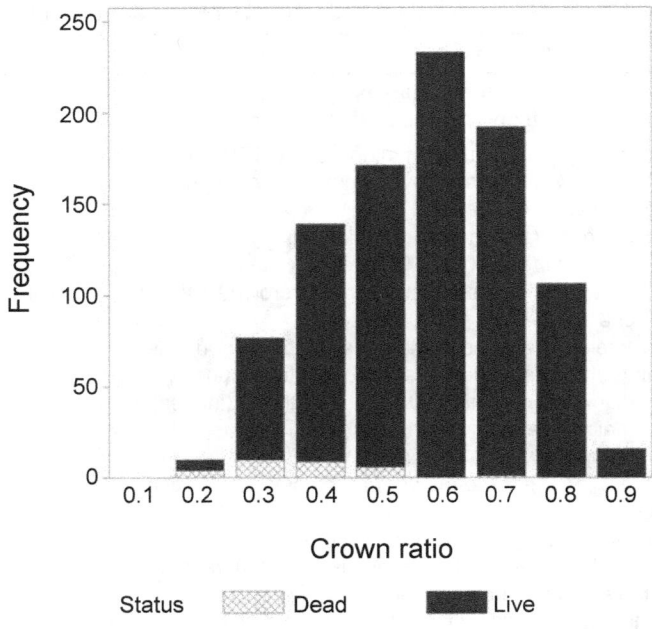

Figure 2. Frequency distribution of crown ratios at the beginning of the study by live/dead status at 5 yrs.

Diameter growth

The dependent variable used to model diameter growth is the natural logarithm of the 5-yr change in squared inside bark diameter [ln(dds)], based on the merits of this transformation (model behavior, accuracy, and validity of statistical assumptions) as discussed by Wykoff (1990). Diameter was measured at breast height, outside bark, but was converted to inside bark by dividing by 1.245 (Johnson 1956). Initial screening of the data indicated possible relationships between ln(dds) and many of the variables listed in Table 3, especially those related to tree size, vigor, and amount of growing space. Data screening also suggested potential dependent variable transformations to explore.

We calculated mean ln(dds) for the five spacings (Table 5). Spacings were significantly different from each other. The influence of more available growing space created by the different thinning intensities was explored in two separate analyses: (1) using actual post-thin density measures (plot and treatment trees/acre and basal area/acre) and (2) using spacing as a class variable. Variables were added into the equation based on improvements in AIC. The equation with density measures can be used to make predictions for any density within the range of our data, while the equation using spacing classes can be used to make predictions for operationally thinned stands that have the same nominal spacings as our study.

Equation with density measures:

$$\ln(dds) = 1.6892 + 0.7725 * \ln(D_0) + 0.1994 * D_0 - 0.3758 * \text{sqrt}(BA_t + 1) + 0.2062 * \text{sqrt}(BA_t + 1) * CR_0 \qquad \text{Eq. 1a}[1]$$

---

[1] A value of 1.0 is added to BA_t to avoid a zero $BA_t * CR_0$ interaction when BA_t is 0.0.

Table 5. Mean 5-yr diameter growth (D_{grow}) and ln(dds)[1] by spacing (ft). Within columns, means followed by the same letter are not statistically different at the P = 0.05 level.

Spacing	D_{grow} (inches)	ln(dds)	N
Control	0.71[a]	0.78[a]	120
5x5	0.89[b]	0.90[a]	179
7x7	1.15[c]	1.41[b]	175
10x10	1.41[d]	1.66[c]	199
14x14	1.77[e]	2.12[d]	195

[1] ln(dds) = natural logarithm of the 5-yr change in squared inside-bark dbh.

Equation with spacing classes:

$$ln(dds) = 0.6112 + 1.0768*ln(D_0) + 0.2733*(D_0) + SPAC + INTER*CR_0$$
$$-1.3607*ln(H_0) + 0.5962*ln(H-5_{grow}) \qquad \text{Eq. 1b}$$

where SPAC and INTER are adjustments to the intercept coefficient for each spacing:

Spacing	SPAC	INTER
Control	0.0	0.1381
5x5	0.0929	0.1973
7x7	0.8154	0.1162
10x10	1.0561	0.1135
14x14	2.0266	-0.0090

The log bias correction factor for Eq. 1a and 1b is 1.527.[2]

Both equations include tree size variables, with predicted diameter growth increasing as tree size increases. Density measures were significant in both equations (BA_t in Eq. 1a and spacing in Eq. 1b), with increasing diameter growth as basal area decreases or as spacings became wider.

Also in both equations, CR_0 is a measure of tree vigor and is included in the equation as an interaction with density. This interaction is easier to interpret in Eq. 1b. The spacing coefficients show that diameter growth increases for all trees with increases in spacing. In addition, the interaction term ($INTER*CR_0$) shows that some spacings have better growth rates as crown ratio increases. The 5x5 spacing has the most rapid increase in diameter growth as crown ratio increases, followed by the control, and then the 7x7 and 10x10. Trees in the 14x14 spacing have the best diameter growth attributable to spacing, but the interaction between crown ratio and spacing is not significant. The interaction between spacing and crown ratio results in the differentiation in tree sizes within some spacings.

---

[2] When transforming predicted values to the original units of measurement, predictions must be multiplied by a log bias correction factor (LBCF) to avoid underestimations (Baskerville 1972). The formula is $LBCF = EXP[X^2/2]$, where X is the standard deviation of the transformed variable. For this equation, average ln(dds) = 1.4352 and the standard deviation is 0.92005; therefore, $LBCF = EXP[(0.92005)^2/2] = 1.527$.

The natural log of 5-yr height growth [$\ln(H_{grow})$] was the dependent variable in the analysis of height growth. The best independent variables were tree size (D_0), beginning crown ratio [$\ln(CR_0)$], pre-thin height growth [$\ln(H\text{-}5_{grow})$], and post-thin treatment basal area (BA_t). The coefficients predicting height growth are shown in Eq. 2. Increases in height growth are associated with increasing initial tree size, larger crown ratios, and increasing 5-yr height growth prior to thinning. Decreases in height growth are associated with increases in post-thin treatment basal area. Shoot borer occurrence was not significant. An alternative equation to predict height growth from spacing was not developed because spacing was not significant.

$$\ln(H_{grow}) = 1.4856 + 0.0917*D_0 + 0.2789*\ln(CR_0) + 0.2335*\ln(H\text{-}5_{grow})$$
$$-0.1372*\ln(BA_t + 1) \qquad \text{Eq. 2}$$

The LBCF for Eq. 2 is 1.079.

Height/diameter ratios

Inter-tree competition restricts diameter growth more severely than height growth, which results in trees that are tall relative to their diameter (Ritchie 1997; Henry and Aarssen 1999). These slender trees are more susceptible to wind and snow damage (Wonn and O'Hara 2001). A measure of slenderness is the height/diameter (H/D) ratio. In this study, initially slender trees reflect the degree of crowding experienced before thinning. Changes in H/D ratios following thinning reflect adjustments to the additional growing space, which could help managers choose the appropriate spacing for their objectives. H/D ratios were calculated using identical units in the numerator and denominator and using dbh. Higher H/D ratios indicate slender trees.

Figure 3 shows H_0/D_0 ratios for all sites. Very short trees have unrealistically high ratios, which indicate that H_0/D_0 ratios are not stable across a range of tree sizes. This

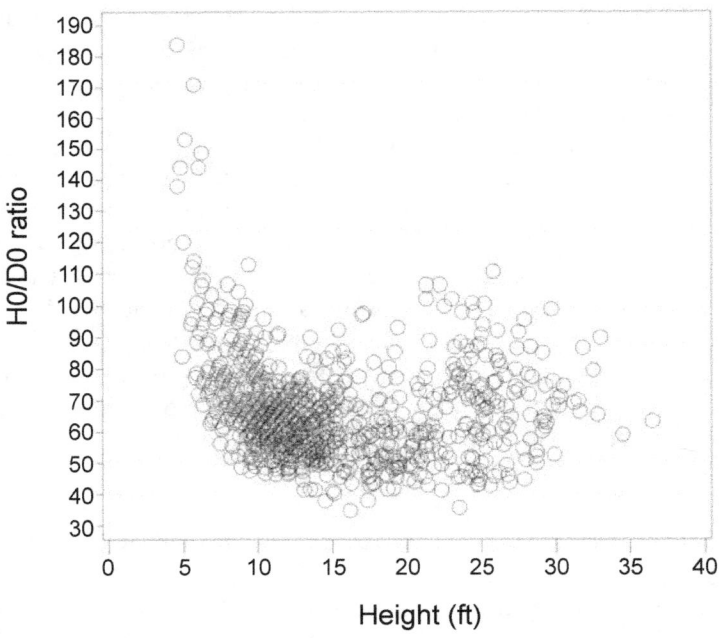

Figure 3. Height/diameter (H_0/D_0) ratios by tree height at the time of thinning.

instability is caused by the numerator of the ratio beginning at 4.5 ft as trees grow past the dbh threshold, while the denominator begins at zero. For this reason, we restricted analyses of H/D ratios to trees ≥8 ft tall at the time of thinning.

Mean H_0/D_0 ratios for sample trees varied from 60.5 for the 14x14 spacing to 69.6 for the 5x5 spacing (Table 6). At narrow spacings, crews left higher numbers of slender trees (higher H_0/D_0 ratios), but as spacing increased, the proportion of trees with lower ratios increased. This is a reasonable result because crews were instructed to leave the best available trees at the approximate spacing for the experimental unit. As spacing decreases, a higher proportion of poor trees must be left to obtain the desired spacing.

Table 6. Mean H/D ratios for sample trees ≥8.0 ft tall at yr 0 (H_0/D_0) and yr 5 (H_5/D_5) by spacing (ft). Means followed by the same letter are not statistically different at the P = 0.05 level.

Spacing	Year	Mean	Std. Dev.	N
Control	0	65.7[ab]	13.7	108
	5	69.6[a]	16.6	108
5x5	0	69.6[a]	13.7	151
	5	69.4[a]	15.8	150
7x7	0	64.8[bc]	12.5	163
	5	61.2[cde]	12.8	162
10x10	0	63.9[bcd]	12.8	183
	5	57.9[e]	12.7	181
14x14	0	60.5[de]	12.2	184
	5	51.2[f]	8.7	183

Five yrs after thinning, mean H_5/D_5 ratios had changed across spacings (Table 6). At narrower spacings, the ratios or variation increased over time, indicating the trees were still crowded and were becoming more slender. At the 10x10 and 14x14 spacings, the ratios and variation decreased.

Graphical results of H_5/D_5 ratios are shown in Figure 4. As spacing increases, there is a large increase in the percentage of trees at a ratio of 60 and lower. Many of the trees in the tighter spacings were still slender, while trees at wider spacings were increasing in diameter relative to height.

We also analyzed ratios for 5-yr height growth divided by 5-yr diameter growth (H_{grow}/D_{grow}), because this ratio may be a more sensitive indicator of tree response to thinning. All trees ≥4.5 ft were used in this analysis. The best predictors of H_{grow}/D_{grow} ratios are spacing, post-thin basal area (BA_t), and beginning crown ratio (CR_0). Mean H_{grow}/D_{grow} ratios decreased with increasing spacing, from 101.5 in the control to 38.2 in the 14x14 treatment (Table 7). The largest change was 31.5 points (50% of the total decrease) between the 5x5 and 7x7 spacings. Similarly, H_{grow}/D_{grow} ratios decreased as beginning crown ratio (CR_0) increased (Table 8). The trees with small crown ratios tended to occur at closer spacings, which meant they were growing at high densities before thinning and were still at relatively high densities after thinning (Table 8).

Change in crown ratios

Crown ratio is calculated using height to crown base and total tree height. Generally, trees released from competition would increase in crown ratio, as the lower branches persist longer and total height increases, unless trees have been so affected by dense conditions that they respond slowly to additional space (Oliver and Larson 1990). We calculated mean change in crown ratio (CR_Δ) for the five spacings (Table 9). The spacings were significantly different, except for the 10x10 and 14x14.

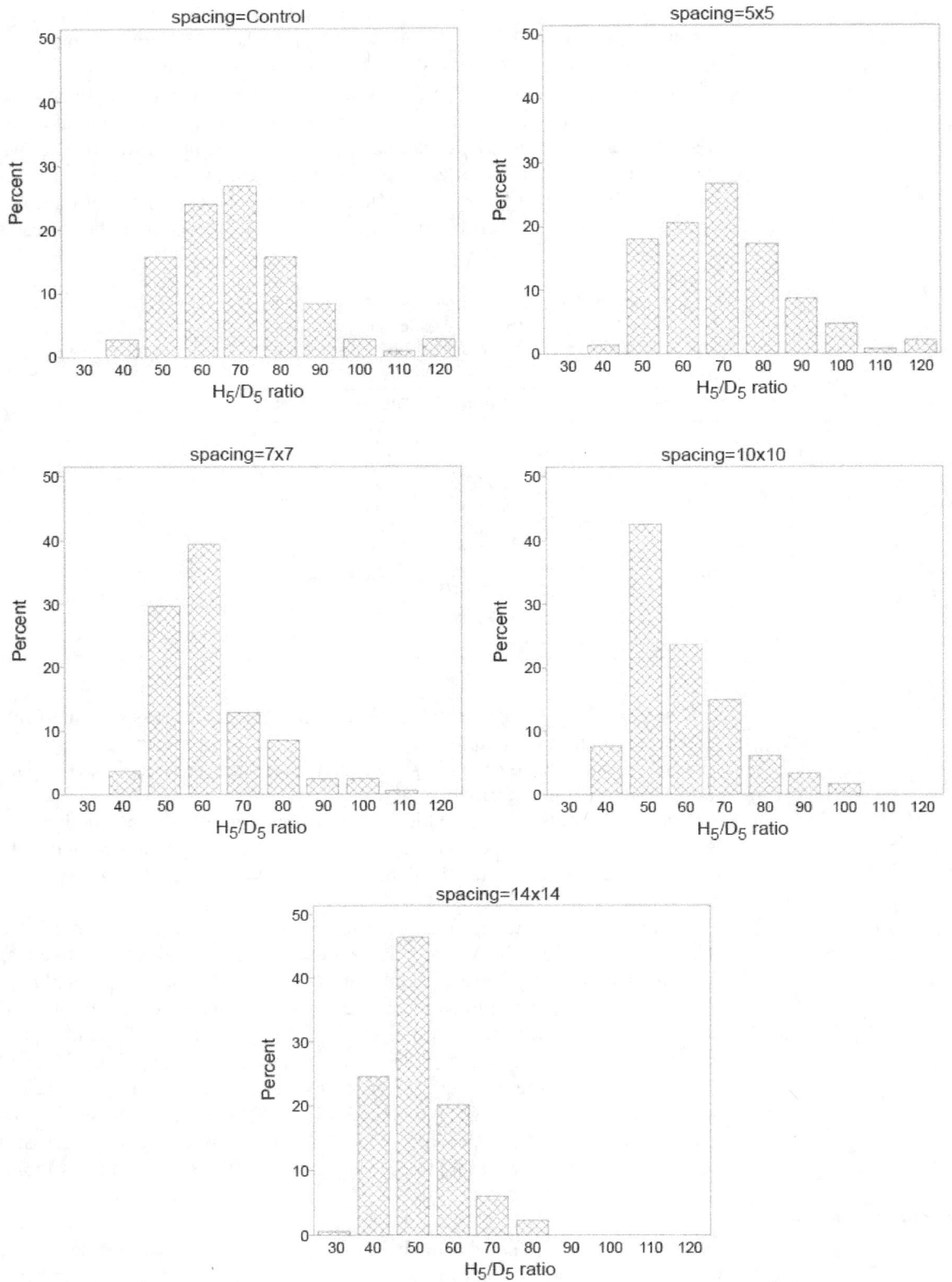

Figure 4. Distribution of height/diameter (H_5/D_5) ratios at yr 5.

USDA Forest Service Res. Pap. RMRS-RP-88. 2011

Table 7. Mean H_{grow}/D_{grow} ratio by spacing (ft). Means followed by the same letter are not statistically different at the P = 0.05 level.

Spacing	H_{grow}/D_{grow}	N
Control	101.5[a]	123
5x5	93.8[a]	183
7x7	62.3[b]	184
10x10	52.0[bc]	198
14x14	38.2[c]	198

Table 8. Mean H_{grow}/D_{grow} ratio by beginning crown ratio (CR_0). Means followed by the same letter are not statistically different at the P = 0.05 level.

CR_0	H_{grow}/D_{grow}	Pre-thin basal area (BA_0)	Post-thin basal area (BA_t)	N
0.2	118[a]	94	35	5
0.3	104[a]	112	50	57
0.4	86[a]	102	48	124
0.5	82[a]	97	44	156
0.6	59[b]	68	36	232
0.7	53[b]	56	30	191
0.8	47[b]	41	24	106
0.9	41[b]	25	27	15

Table 9. Mean CR_Δ by spacing (ft). Means followed by the same letter are not statistically different at the P = 0.05 level.

Spacing	CR_Δ	N
Control	-0.117[a]	122
5x5	-0.065[b]	183
7x7	-0.037[c]	174
10x10	-0.002[d]	198
14x14	0.010[d]	194

We modeled change in crown ratio (CR_Δ) based on independent variables determined from initial screening of the data. The influence of increased growing space after thinning was explored with separate analyses, one with measures of post-thin density and one with spacing as a class variable.

Equation with density measures:

$$CR_\Delta = 0.5211 - 0.5027*CR_{HCB} - 0.06347*\ln(BA_t + 1)$$ Eq. 3a

Equation with spacing classes:

$$CR_\Delta = 0.1979 - 0.4485*CR_{HCB} + SPAC$$ Eq. 3b

where SPAC is an adjustment to the intercept coefficient specific to each spacing level:

SPAC	Coefficient
Control	0.0
5x5	0.0296
7x7	0.0710
10x10	0.1028
14x14	0.1291

Both equations include a coefficient for beginning crown ratio (CR_{HCB}) and a measure of density. For both equations, as CR_{HCB} increases, CR_Δ decreases. And for any fixed CR_{HCB}, tighter spacing results in a decrease in CR_Δ.

Height to crown base

The height to crown base (HCB) is defined as the lowest whorl in the crown that has at least two live branches. HCB is important because low crown bases increase the risk of tree torching and crown fires, while higher HCB values mean there is greater distance between the ground and base of the crown. A low canopy base height makes crown fire initiation easier (Scott and Reinhardt 2001). Also, crown retention has important implications for wood quality. We analyzed height to base of crown to (1) determine if HCB changed following spacing (HCB_Δ); (2) determine if HCB tended to change by spacing or, conversely, if there was large tree-to-tree variation in HCB within spacings; and (3) to predict HCB_Δ for the first 5 yrs after thinning.

Table 10 shows attributes for HCB by spacing, and Figure 5 shows the decline in HCB_Δ as spacing increases for the seven sites. There is a clear increase in HCB_Δ at denser spacings, tapering off to smaller increases at wider spacings. When all sites are combined, HCB_Δ increased 3.5 ft in the control, 2.7 ft in the 5x5, 2.2 ft in the 7x7, 1.7 ft in the 10x10, and 1.3 ft in the 14x14. Therefore, narrower spacings resulted in higher crown bases than wider spacings.

Table 10. Mean change in 5-yr height to crown base (HCB_Δ) and heights to crown base by year and spacing (ft). Within columns, means followed by the same letter are not statistically different at the P = 0.05 level.

Spacing	Mean HCB_Δ (ft)	Mean HCB_0 (ft)	Mean HCB_5 (ft)
Control	3.5[a]	4.6[a]	8.0[a]
5x5	2.7[b]	4.9[a]	7.6[ab]
7x7	2.2[c]	4.8[a]	7.0[abc]
10x10	1.7[d]	4.9[a]	6.6[bc]
14x14	1.3[e]	4.8[a]	6.1[c]

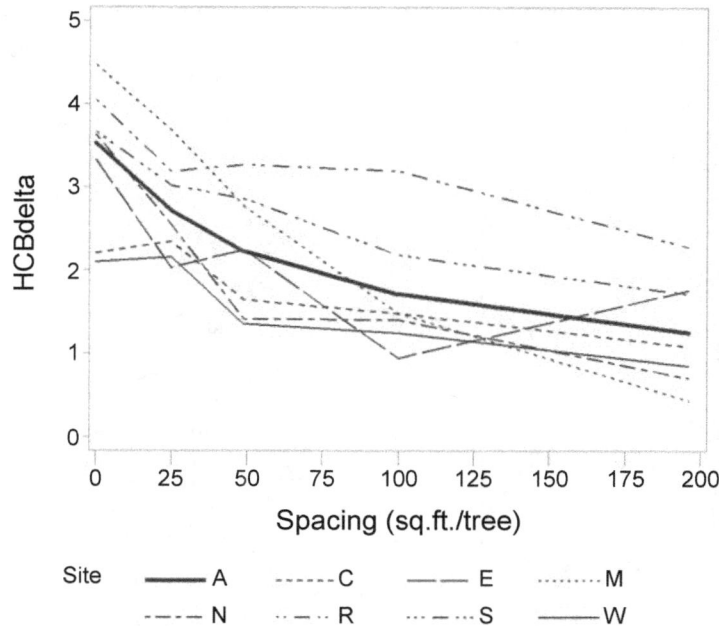

Figure 5. Average change in height to crown base (HCB$_\Delta$) by site and spacing: A = all sites, C = Cold Springs, E = East Castle Rock, M = Mosquito Heights, N = North Talmaks, R = Reubens, S = South Castle Rock, W = West Talmaks.

We calculated and plotted cumulative HCB$_0$ and HCB$_5$ distributions by spacing (Figure 6), which shows what can be expected for these types of operationally thinned stands. The control had the largest increase in HCB, followed by progressively smaller increases at wider spacings. Differences between HCB$_0$ and HCB$_5$ can be used to estimate the percentage of crowns that will be above a given height as a result of thinning to a particular spacing, which should be useful in determining spacings that have HCB values above wildfire or prescribed fire torching heights.

Regression analysis showed that beginning crown ratio (CR$_0$), post-thin treatment basal area (BA$_t$), and beginning diameter (D$_0$) were the best variables for predicting HCB$_\Delta$. Increases in HCB$_\Delta$ were associated with larger initial crown ratios, increasing treatment basal area or spacing, and larger initial tree diameter.

Equation with density measures:

$$HCB_\Delta = -0.7507 +2.5305*CR_0 +0.0301*BA_t +0.2077*sqrt(D_0) \qquad \text{Eq. 4a}$$

Equation with spacing classes:

$$HCB_\Delta = 1.4645 +1.1790*CR_0 +0.8525*sqrt(D_0) +SPAC \qquad \text{Eq. 4b}$$

where SPAC is an adjustment to the intercept coefficient for each spacing level:

SPAC	Coefficient
Control	0.0
5x5	-0.6414
7x7	-1.2283
10x10	-1.8309
14x14	-2.3880

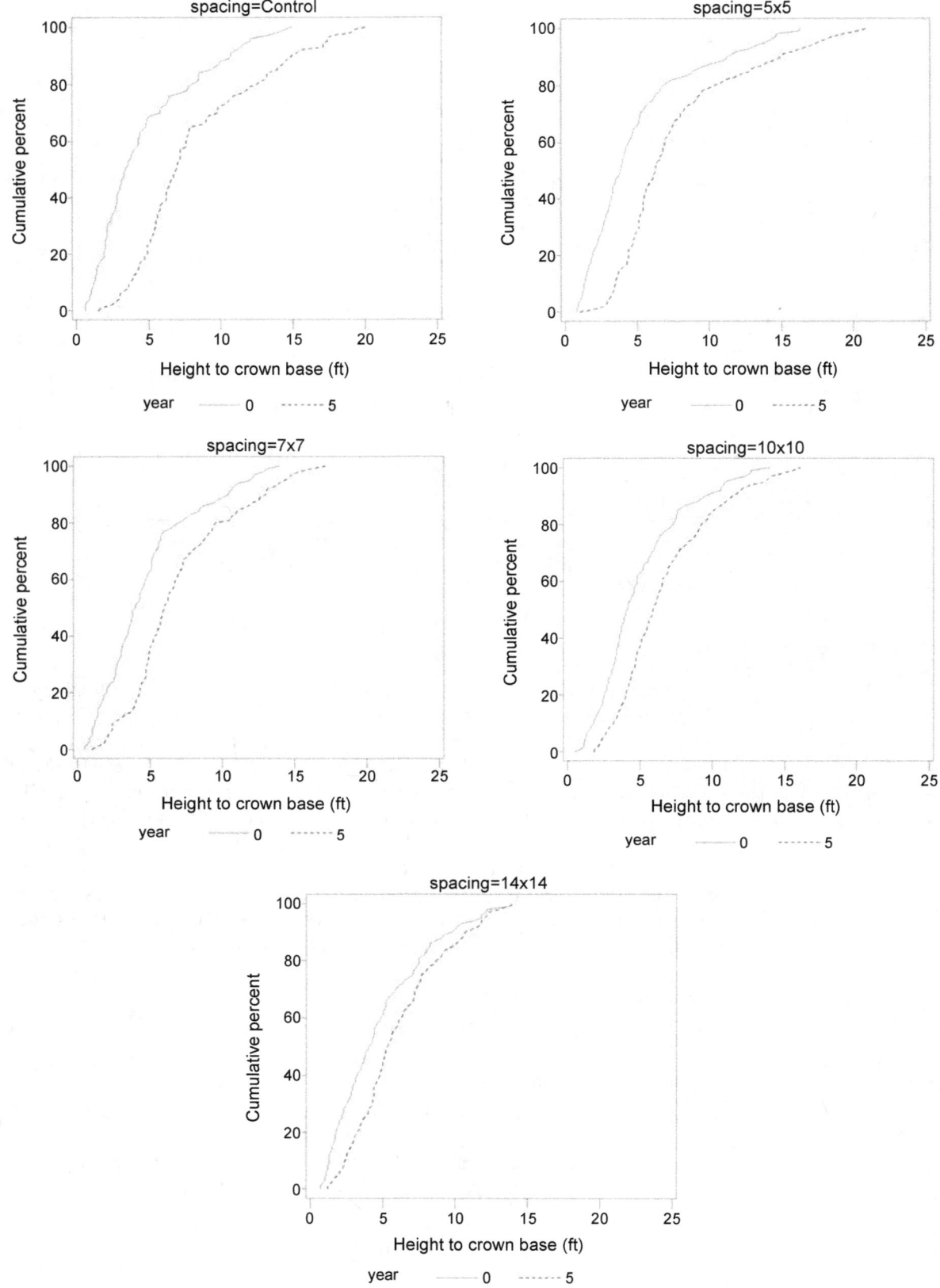

Figure 6. Cumulative percentage height to crown base (HCB) distributions.

USDA Forest Service Res. Pap. RMRS-RP-88. 2011

Shoot borer damage

A total of 245 trees (27.1%) had shoot borer damage during the 5 yrs after thinning. The probability of shoot borer damage is predicted as a continuous value bounded in the interval [0,1] using the logistic equation $1/(1+e^{-\sum \beta_i X_i})$ where "e" is the base of natural logarithms, ß are regression coefficients, and X are independent variables.

Study site elevation (E) had the highest predictive value, with the probability of shoot borer damage decreasing with increasing elevation. The next best predictor was 5-yr height growth prior to thinning (H-5$_{grow}$), which was positively associated with shoot borer damage. Beginning crown ratio (CR$_0$) was also positively associated with shoot borer damage. Finally, post-treatment basal area (BA$_t$) was inversely related to the probability of shoot borer damage. The equation is:

$$\text{Prob} = 1/(1+e-(-0.5467 -0.00075*E +0.6612*\ln(\text{H-5}_{grow}) +1.2225*\text{CR}_0 -0.0085*\text{BA}_t)) \qquad \text{Eq. 5}$$

An alternative equation to predict shoot borer damage from spacing was not developed because spacing was not significant.

Non-Tree Vegetation and Thinning Slash

The forbs and shrubs that occurred on the study sites are very typical for these habitat types. There are differences in species composition between the Nez Perce and Spokane Tribal lands, but these differences relate to habitat types. Species acronyms, common names, and scientific names are given in Table 11, while occurrence for forb and shrub species is shown in Table 12 by study site. Species that are fairly common across all study sites are common yarrow, clustered frasera, thistles, vetch, serviceberry, black hawthorn, roses, spiraea, and snowberry. Forbs common on wetter sites are strawberry, northern bedstraw, sweetscented bedstraw, old man's whiskers, sticky purple geranium, hawkweed, Brewer's mitrewort, mountain sweet-cicely, and penstemon. Field bindweed, coast tarweed, and spotted knapweed have high occurrence at the two Castle Rock sites, which are the driest sites in the study. The decrease in spotted knapweed at the two Castle Rock sites between yrs 1 and 5 (Table 12) is attributed to release of biological control agents (*Bangasternus fausti* in 2001 and *Larinus minutus* in 2002). Both agents are weevils that feed on flower heads of spotted knapweed.

The forb species that had the highest occurrences are shown for yr 1 and 5 in Table 13. Some species had increased occurrence at wider spacings, some species had decreased occurrence at narrower spacings, some species increased at all spacings, and some species had no discernable pattern.

Epilobium (species other than fireweed, *Epilobium angustifolium*) had increased occurrence as spacing increased. There was no change in the control, +5% in the 5x5 spacing, +14% in the 7x7, +14% in the 10x10, and +23% in the 14x14. Similar responses of increased occurrence at wider spacings were found for vetch and, to a lesser extent, for field bindweed, Gairdner's yampa, cinquefoil, and penstemon.

Strawberry had a 14% decrease from yr 1 to yr 5 in the control, but was fairly stable over time at all spacings. Thistle had 8 to 11% decreases in the 5x5, 10x10, and 14x14 spacings, but no change in the 7x7 and control. Coast tarweed was not found in any spacings in yr 1 after the thinning but had the highest occurrence of any forb by yr 5. Coast tarweed occurred more often at the three wider spacings (29% in the 7x7, 20% in the 10x10, and 29% in the 14x14), but less often in the control (11%) and 5x5 (14%). Also, dandelion had increases at all spacings, varying from 11 to 20%.

Table 11. Acronym, common name, and scientific name for plant species.

Acronym	Common name	Scientific name
Forbs		
ACMI	Common yarrow	*Achillea millefolium*
CEST	Spotted knapweed	*Centaurea stoebe*
COAR	Field bindweed	*Convolvulus arvensis*
EPAN	Fireweed	*Epilobium angustifolium*
EPSP	Epilobium	*Epilobium* species other than EPAN
ERSP	Daisy	*Erigeron* species
FORB	Forbs	All forb species
FRAG	Strawberry	*Fragaria virginiana* (92%) and *F. vesca* (8%)
FRFA	Clustered frasera	*Frasera fastigiata*
GABO	Northern bedstraw	*Galium boreale*
GATR	Sweetscented bedstraw	*Galium triflorum*
GETR	Old man's whiskers	*Geum triflorum*
GEVI	Sticky purple geranium	*Geranium viscosissimum*
GRAS	Grass and sedge species	Grasses and sedges
HIAL	Hawkweed	*Hieracium albertinum* and *H. albiflorum*
LUPN	Lupine	*Lupine* species
MASA	Coast tarweed	*Madia sativa*
MIBR	Brewer's mitrewort	*Mitella breweri*
OSCH	Mountain sweet-cicely	*Osmorhiza chilensis*
PESP	Penstemon	*Penstemon* species
PEGA	Gairdner's yampa	*Perideridia gairdneri*
POGR	Cinquefoil	*Potentilla gracilis*
TAOF	Dandelion	*Taraxacum officinale*
THIS	Thistle	Thistle (*Cirsium*) species
THOC	Western meadowrue	*Thalictrum occidentale*
TRDU	Western salsify	*Tragopogon dubius*
VTCH	Vetch	Vetch (mostly *Vicia americana*)
Shrubs		
AMAL	Serviceberry	*Amelanchier alnifolia*
BEAQ	Tall Oregon grape	*Berberis aquifolium*
CEVE	Shinyleaf ceanothus	*Ceanothus velutinus*
CRDO	Black hawthorn	*Crataegus douglasii*
HODI	Oceanspray	*Holodiscus discolor*
PHMA	Ninebark	*Physocarpus malvaceus*
PRVI	Common chokecherry	*Prunus virginiana*
RICE	Wax current	*Ribes cereum*
ROSA	Rose species	*Rosa* species
SALX	Willow species	*Salix* species
SPBE	Spiraea	*Spiraea betulifolia*
SYAL	Common snowberry	*Symphoricarpos albus*
Other		
SLAS	Thinned p-pine slash	n/a

Table 12. Average percent occurrence by species and site. The first number in each box is for yr 1 and the second number is for yr 5. The definitions for species acronyms are given in Table 11.

Species	Cold Springs		Reubens		West Talmaks		North Talmaks		South Castle Rock		East Castle Rock		Mosquito Heights	
Forbs														
ACMI	60	76	16	28	72	64	4	12	16	32	16	8	4	4
CEST	0	0	0	0	0	0	0	0	88	52	96	16	0	0
COAR	0	0	0	0	0	0	0	0	76	88	36	52	0	0
EPAN	4	4	0	0	36	32	0	4	0	0	0	0	0	0
EPSP	0	4	0	0	4	4	0	0	8	20	16	72	0	4
ERSP	0	12	4	16	0	8	0	0	0	0	0	0	0	0
FORB	100	100	100	100	100	100	100	100	100	100	100	100	100	100
FRAG	64	44	0	8	76	80	24	8	0	0	0	0	28	40
FRFA	28	28	0	0	20	40	20	24	44	52	8	8	12	0
GABO	64	88	0	0	72	80	8	32	0	0	0	0	0	0
GATR	0	0	0	0	0	0	0	0	0	0	0	0	0	4
GETR	16	24	0	0	28	48	0	12	0	0	0	0	0	0
GEVI	12	44	0	0	68	60	16	20	0	0	0	0	4	0
GRAS	100	100	100	100	100	100	100	100	96	100	48	100	88	100
HIAL	12	16	0	0	28	16	0	4	0	0	0	0	0	0
LUPN	0	20	0	0	0	24	0	0	0	12	0	4	0	8
MASA	0	0	0	0	0	0	0	0	0	52	0	68	0	24
MIBR	0	0	0	0	24	16	8	0	0	0	0	0	0	0
OSCH	20	16	0	4	8	0	0	0	0	0	0	0	0	0
PESP	40	60	0	0	64	56	24	12	0	0	0	0	0	12
PEGA	0	16	0	0	0	32	12	20	0	0	0	0	0	0
POGR	44	16	4	4	12	60	4	24	0	0	0	0	0	8
TAOF	0	0	0	48	0	16	0	12	0	24	0	0	8	12
THIS	32	36	8	0	20	32	12	8	12	0	0	0	24	0
THOC	0	0	0	0	4	16	0	12	0	0	0	0	0	0
TRDU	0	8	4	8	4	4	0	0	4	32	0	4	4	0
VTCH	60	56	4	12	0	0	20	36	4	32	12	60	0	0
Shrubs														
AMAL	4	24	56	76	72	88	12	32	0	24	4	4	36	76
BEAQ	0	0	0	0	0	0	0	0	0	0	0	0	4	4
CEVE	0	0	0	0	0	0	0	0	0	0	0	0	16	8
CRDO	0	8	28	28	0	12	4	4	0	4	0	4	24	64
HODI	12	20	0	0	0	0	0	0	0	0	0	0	12	20
PHMA	4	0	0	0	0	0	0	0	0	0	0	0	4	4
PRVI	0	0	0	0	0	0	20	20	0	0	0	0	32	36
RICE	32	36	0	0	0	0	0	0	0	0	0	0	0	0
ROSA	64	84	8	12	92	96	76	72	0	0	0	0	40	64
SALX	0	0	0	0	0	0	4	0	0	0	0	0	0	4
SPBE	0	0	8	12	12	4	72	68	0	4	4	0	44	60
SYAL	100	100	4	8	96	100	96	100	44	56	12	28	100	100

Table 13. Average percent occurrence of forb species along line intercept transects having a minimum of 20 occurrences by spacing (ft). Definitions for species acronyms are given in Table 11.

Species	Control			5x5			7x7			10x10			14x14		
	1	5	5-1[1]	1	5	5-1	1	5	5-1	1	5	5-1	1	5	5-1
ACMI	14	20	6	23	29	6	31	37	6	31	29	-2	34	49	14
CEST[2]	26	11	-15	26	9	-17	26	6	-20	26	11	-15	29	11	-17
COAR	23	20	-3	20	26	6	20	20	0	11	17	6	6	17	11
EPAN	3	6	3	6	9	3	11	9	-2	9	6	-3	0	0	0
EPSP	6	6	0	6	11	5	0	14	14	3	17	14	3	26	23
FRAG	31	17	-14	26	23	-3	29	29	0	34	29	-5	31	31	0
FRFA	17	23	6	34	26	-8	17	23	6	9	23	14	17	14	-3
GABO	11	23	12	23	26	3	20	31	11	26	34	8	23	29	6
GETR	6	11	5	3	11	8	11	20	9	6	9	3	6	11	6
GEVI	9	17	8	11	14	3	17	17	0	14	20	6	20	20	0
MASA	0	11	11	0	14	14	0	29	29	0	20	20	0	29	29
PEGA	0	3	3	0	11	11	0	9	9	0	14	14	9	11	3
PESP	23	17	-6	31	29	-2	23	29	6	6	9	3	9	17	8
POGR	0	6	6	11	20	9	11	26	15	14	14	0	9	20	11
TAOF	3	17	14	3	23	20	0	11	11	0	17	17	0	11	11
THIS	14	14	0	14	6	-8	11	11	0	17	9	-8	26	14	-11
VTCH	14	17	3	11	20	9	9	23	14	17	37	20	23	40	17
FORB	80	90	10	97	94	-3	87	90	3	91	94	3	91	97	6
GRAS	100	93	-7	100	97	-3	100	90	-10	100	100	0	100	100	0
SLAS	n/a	n/a	n/a	81	78	-3	87	90	3	94	94	0	94	94	0

[1] Yr 5 minus yr 1.
[2] Decline is attributed to two introduced biological control insects. See text for details.

Only six shrub species were abundant enough for analysis of occurrence, percent cover, and height; and few of these attributes changed with spacings from yr 1 to yr 5 (Table 14). Serviceberry occurrence varied from 20 to 37% in yr 1, increasing to 40 to 54% in yr 5, but these changes were not significant. The average increase in occurrence across all spacing for serviceberry was 20%, but the control increased about the same. Cover and height of serviceberry changed little between yrs 1 and 5.

Black hawthorn occurrence varied from 9 to 14% in yr 1, increasing to 11 to 31% in yr 5, but these changes were not significant (Table 14). Cover and height of black hawthorn changed little between yrs 1 and 5. Chokecherry occurrence varied from 0 to 14% in yrs 1 and 5, with essentially no increase in occurrence. Percent cover did increase consistently for the three wider spacings, but by less than 4% (not significant). Roses had overall high occurrence, which varied from 31 to 49% in yr 1 and increased slightly to 40 to 57% in yr 5, but these changes were not significant. Average change in rose cover showed some significant differences between spacings, but increases in height were not significantly different.

Spiraea increased slightly in occurrence, cover, and height between yrs 1 and 5, but there were no significant differences between spacings. Snowberry had the highest occurrence of all shrub species, averaging 60 to 69% in yr 1, with minor increases to 66 to 77% in yr 5. Percent cover of snowberry was also the highest of all shrub species, averaging 19 to 24% in yr 1 and 20 to 25% in yr 5. Changes in snowberry occurrence, cover, and height were not significantly different between spacings.

The bottom of Table 14 shows a summary for all shrubs, which includes species other than the six listed in the upper part of the table. Percent cover for all shrubs is the summation of cover for each shrub species on the plot, which could exceed 100% due to overlapping crowns. There is a small increase in shrub occurrence (averaging 7.8 %) and percent cover (averaging 3.7%) but no patterns related to spacing.

Table 14. Average occurrence, cover, and height of shrub species by spacing (ft). Within species and variable (occurrence, cover, or height), means followed by the same letter are not statistically different at the P = 0.05 level. Definitions for species acronyms are given in Table 11.

Species	Spacing	Occurrence (%) 1	5	5-1[1]	Cover (%)[2] 1	5	5-1[1]	Height (ft)[2] 1	5	5-1[1]
AMAL	Control	20	43	23[a]	1.87	3.80	1.93[a]	1.10	1.52	0.42[a]
	5x5	37	54	17[a]	2.00	2.42	0.42[a]	1.11	1.18	0.07[a]
	7x7	26	40	14[a]	2.50	3.43	0.93[a]	1.01	1.82	0.81[a]
	10x10	20	49	29[a]	1.65	3.59	1.94[a]	1.52	2.24	0.72[a]
	14x14	29	46	17[a]	1.63	3.44	1.81[a]	1.03	2.07	1.04[a]
CRDO	Control	9	20	11[a]	2.43	4.29	1.86[a]	1.97	3.60	1.63[a]
	5x5	9	11	2[a]	*	*	*	*	*	*
	7x7	14	31	17[a]	0.45	1.00	0.55[a]	0.51	1.25	0.74[a]
	10x10	9	11	2[a]	*	*	*	*	*	*
	14x14	9	14	5[a]	0.60	1.00	0.40[a]	0.56	1.18	0.62[a]
PRVI	Control	3	6	3[a]	*	*	*	*	*	*
	5x5	0	0	0[a]						
	7x7	14	14	0[a]	5.20	8.40	3.20[a]	1.84	2.66	0.82[a]
	10x10	6	6	0[a]	*	*	*	*	*	*
	14x14	14	14	0[a]	4.40	8.20	3.80[a]	2.67	2.33	-0.34[a]
ROSA	Control	40	40	0[a]	1.86	3.36	1.50[a]	1.24	1.51	0.27[a]
	5x5	49	57	8[a]	1.45	1.20	-0.25[c]	0.67	0.98	0.31[a]
	7x7	43	46	3[a]	1.63	1.50	-0.13[bc]	0.93	1.09	0.16[a]
	10x10	34	40	6[a]	1.07	1.86	0.79[abc]	0.77	1.08	0.31[a]
	14x14	31	51	20[a]	1.22	2.44	1.22[ab]	0.76	1.27	0.51[a]
SPBE	Control	23	29	6[a]	3.30	4.00	0.70[a]	0.67	0.67	0.0[a]
	5x5	20	23	3[a]	2.38	3.00	0.62[a]	0.55	0.64	0.09[a]
	7x7	20	23	3[a]	6.50	7.50	1.00[a]	0.43	0.78	0.35[a]
	10x10	26	20	-6[a]	1.43	1.57	0.14[a]	0.68	0.75	0.07[a]
	14x14	11	11	0[a]	*	*	*	*	*	*
SYAL	Control	66	77	11[a]	21.74	21.15	-0.59[a]	1.55	1.42	-0.13[a]
	5x5	69	69	0[a]	22.25	24.71	2.46[a]	1.39	1.52	0.13[a]
	7x7	69	69	0[a]	18.75	20.33	1.58[a]	1.48	1.48	0.0[a]
	10x10	60	66	6[a]	24.43	25.09	0.66[a]	1.25	1.34	0.09[a]
	14x14	60	71	11[a]	21.84	19.40	-2.44[a]	1.27	1.31	0.04[a]
Shrubs	Control	74	86	12	22.47	27.61	5.14			
	5x5	83	89	6	21.67	22.77	1.10			
	7x7	80	83	3	21.16	25.65	4.49			
	10x10	74	80	6	19.61	23.83	4.22			
	14x14	74	86	12	24.27	27.63	3.36			

[1] Yr 5 minus yr 1.
[2] Mean for those plots on which the species occurred by yr 5; if the species did not occur on the plot in yr 1, cover and height were assigned a value of zero for yr 1.
*Fewer than 5 plots available to calculate the mean.

As shown in Table 13, forb and grass occurrence was always high, averaging at least 80% occurrence for forbs and at least 90% for grasses. Forb coverage did not change appreciably (≤2%) between yr 1 and yr 5 (Table 15). Grass coverage decreased in all spacings between yr 1 and yr 5, from -5% in the 7x7 spacing to -11% in the 5x5. The control and 5x5, which had the highest values at yr 1, had the largest declines in coverage of grass.

Table 15. Average percent cover of forbs, grasses, and ponderosa pine thinning slash along line intercept transects for plots where the species occurs by spacing (ft).

Variable	Spacing	Yr 1 (%)	Yr 5 (%)	5-1[1] (%)
Forb	Control	7	5	-2
	5x5	7	9	2
	7x7	9	9	0
	10x10	7	7	0
	14x14	7	6	-1
Grass	Control	25	15	-10
	5x5	23	12	-11
	7x7	19	14	-5
	10x10	19	12	-7
	14x14	17	8	-9
SLAS	Control	n/a	n/a	n/a
	5x5	9	4	-5
	7x7	11	6	-5
	10x10	17	8	-9
	14x14	13	7	-6

[1]Yr 5 minus yr 1.

Ponderosa pine thinning slash was recorded on the line transects. Highest occurrences were in the wider spacings, starting at ~80% for the 5x5, ~90% for the 7x7, and 94% for the 10x10 and 14x14 (Table 13). The measurement of slash in yr 1 included stems, branches, and foliage. By yr 5, foliage had fallen off the branches and was mostly incorporated into the duff layer. Therefore, average percent cover of ponderosa pine thinning slash decreased between 5 and 9% from yr 1 to yr 5 (Table 15, Figure 7).

Discussion

Data for this study came from naturally regenerated, operationally thinned-from-below stands. Thinning crews chose the best available trees at the approximate spacing that was randomly chosen for the experimental unit. Thinning from below results in the "selection effect" (discussed by Hynynen 1995) or the "chainsaw effect," meaning that leave trees in stands that are thinned from below grew better before thinning compared to those removed during thinning. In our study, there is a second component to the selection effect because of pre-thin heterogeneity in tree sizes and vigor. With a variety of tree sizes and vigor to choose from, it is expected that there would be a higher proportion of larger, better trees at wider spacings than at narrower spacings. This happened because at narrower spacings, crews had no choice but to leave smaller, low vigor trees; while at wider spacings, there were generally enough large, better vigor trees to meet spacing requirements. Therefore, mean tree characteristics vary with spacing immediately

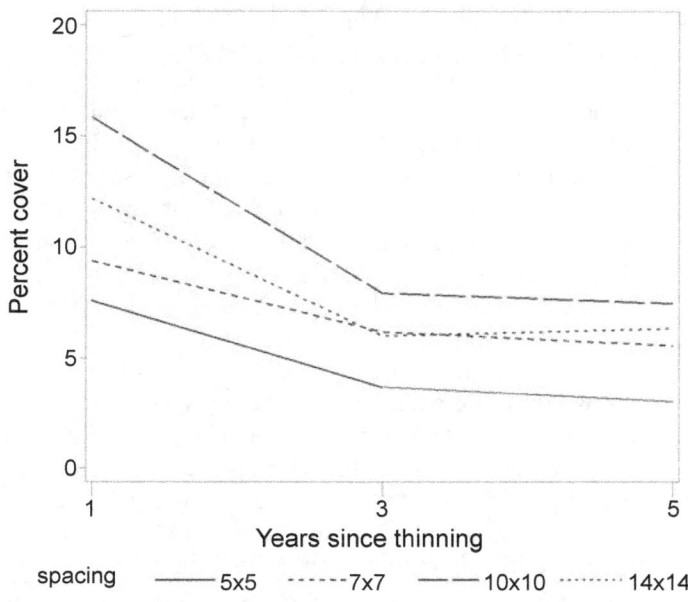

Figure 7. Percent cover of ponderosa pine thinning slash over time by spacing.

after thinning. Our analyses that used individual tree characteristics allow prediction for stands that may differ from ours in terms of tree sizes, H/D ratios, crown ratios, etc.

Thinning studies differ from plantation spacing studies because in plantation spacing studies, tree size and vigor are similar across spacings, and spacings can be rigidly controlled. Thinning studies are less likely to meet the designated densities. Even if dense areas are rigidly spaced, understocked or non-stocked patches within treatments will result in wider average spacings than specified, which appeared to be the case in the 5x5 and 7x7 spacings (Table 2).

Trees

Severe lean and mortality

Trees that were classified as having severe lean following thinning were those we considered unable to recover and grow vertically. Only 15 trees (1.6%) developed severe lean, showing that the vast majority of trees did not have problems remaining upright after thinning, even though pre-thin densities averaged from 2,469 trees/acre at Reubens to 10,128 trees/acre at East Castle Rock. Few trees died following the thinning (30 trees or 3.1%). Those trees that died had smaller crown ratios, were growing slower relative to other trees, and had higher H_0/D_0 ratios (slender trees). Therefore, severe lean or tree death following thinning does not seem to be a major concern for ponderosa pine on these dry sites where snowloads are not generally a problem. However, our results should be used with caution because snowloads can differ between areas and between different years.

Our results agree with other research. Ronco and others (1985) found little tree damage and mortality in a sapling- and pole-size ponderosa pine thinning experiment in northern Arizona, except for some snow damage the first spring after thinning. About 12% of the trees had snow damage and were removed; these trees were the smaller trees in their study. Cochran and Barrett (1999) attributed all mortality in their study to mountain pine beetle (*Dendroctonus ponderosae*) in a pole-size ponderosa pine thinning study in central Oregon. Those naturally regenerated trees averaged 48 ft tall at the time of treatment, compared to 14.5 ft tall in our study. Even though the trees sampled by Cochran and Barrett (1999) only averaged 25% crown ratio, the authors reported no snow or wind damage following thinning. Barrett (1982) reported that mortality was minor in thinned ponderosa pine trees that were about 1 inch dbh and 8 ft tall at the time of thinning. No mortality occurred at the widest spacings, and most of the mortality was in the smallest diameter class.

Diameter growth

Diameter growth (D_{grow}) was greatly influenced by spacing—widely spaced trees grew faster in diameter than narrowly spaced trees. Also, larger trees, as measured by beginning dbh (D_0), had faster diameter growth, and trees with larger beginning crown ratios (CR_0) had faster diameter growth. Our results showing higher diameter growth being associated with larger trees and trees with larger crown ratios agrees with other research (e.g., Wykoff 1986; Wagner and Radosevich 1991; Hynynen 1995). Larger trees are in a more dominant position than smaller trees. Beginning crown ratio is an indicator of pre-thin conditions, likely serving as a surrogate for stand density (Garber and others 2008). Trees with larger crown ratios have the photosynthetic capacity to support faster growth rates.

There is good agreement that lower densities result in faster diameter growth for ponderosa pine (Meyer 1934; Oliver 1979; Barrett 1982; Ronco and others 1985; Oliver 1997) and for other species that can grow in the Inland Northwest (Johnstone 1981; Reukema and Smith 1987; Harrington and others 2009).

Height growth

Five-yr post-thin height growth was not related to spacing. Height growth was better for larger diameter trees (D_0), trees with larger crown ratios (CR_0), and trees with better pre-thin height growth (H-5$_{grow}$). Height growth decreased with increasing post-thin treatment basal area (BA_t). For seedlings and saplings in this study, it was typical that larger trees in the size classes grew more rapidly than smaller trees (Wykoff 1986; Reukema and Smith 1987; Ferguson 1988; Wagner and Radosevich 1991; Uzoh and Oliver 2006). Smaller pre-thin crown ratios indicated competition that had prevented trees from developing fuller crowns, which meant these trees needed time to build crowns following thinning in order to support normal growth. Lower pre-thin height growth was an indication of competition, poor microsites, or genetic variation within species.

Post-thin treatment basal area (BA_t) was a significant predictor of height growth, but spacing (SPAC) was not. SPAC and BA_t are two different measures of competition. SPAC indicates the approximate amount of growing space for each tree, regardless of tree size. BA_t includes the basal area attributed to competing trees on the 1/400-acre plot, plus any trees in the variable radius plot. Trees in the variable radius plot were greater than or equal to 2.3 inches dbh and contribute to BA_t more than small-diameter trees on the 1/400-acre plot because the contribution of each tree to BA_t is proportional to diameter squared. Therefore, higher BA_t values indicate that the subject tree was likely receiving competition from larger trees, whereas SPAC does not imply anything about size of competing trees.

There is fairly good agreement in the scientific literature that height growth of trees is not influenced by spacing, except at very high or very low densities. Lanner (1985) reviewed literature for several species and provided explanations for height growth insensitivity to spacing and diameter growth sensitivity to spacing. Specific to ponderosa pine, Oliver (1984) found that height growth of trees in a thinned plantation of saplings in northern California was not influenced by spacing, and Oliver (1990) found that height growth of planted ponderosa pine was not influenced by spacing on the west slope of the Sierra Nevada Mountains. Meyer (1934) noted that in cutover ponderosa pine forests of the Pacific Northwest, increased diameter growth was not accompanied by increased height growth.

However, there is also contradictory evidence on the generality that spacing does not influence height growth. Ronco and others (1985) found that annual height growth of ponderosa pine decreased with increasing basal area during the first 10-yr period after thinning in northern Arizona, but basal area was not significant during the second 10-yr period. They attributed the significant negative association between height growth and basal area to the removal of shorter trees of poor form during thinning, rather than to increased height growth with lower stand densities. This is an example of the selection effect cited by Hynynen (1995).

Barrett (1982) found that thinned ponderosa pine had better height increments at wider spacings in central Oregon. Although significant, Barrett cautioned that the trees had been very suppressed by high sapling densities and an overstory, and were growing only a few inches in height per year before thinning. It may have been possible that released saplings were able to respond more rapidly at the wider spacings, while adjustments were taking longer at narrower spacings.

Van Deusen (1968) reported that average height growth of ponderosa pine in the Black Hills of South Dakota was always greater for trees in thinned stands versus unthinned stands. The length of the height growth period was similar between thinned and unthinned stands; however, density could be confounded with tree size at the time of treatment because trees in the thinned stand averaged 5.2 inch dbh while trees in the unthinned stand averaged 3.5 inch dbh. This, too, appears to be an example of the selection effect.

Results from plantation spacing trials may be relevant to detecting density effects on height growth. Oliver (1997) found that height growth was weakly related to density in a ponderosa pine plantation thinned to five stocking levels. There was a decline in height growth from low density to high density, but this relationship was only significant in the first two of the five 5-yr growth periods. Reukema and Smith (1987) found that plantation spacing had little effect on heights of Douglas-fir (*Pseudotsuga menziesii*), western redcedar (*Thuja plicata*), or western hemlock (*Tsuga heterophylla*). Harrington and others (2009) found no spacing differences in Douglas-fir plantations for 3-yr height or 25-yr top height. Reukema (1979) found that, on better sites, plantation spacing had little effect on height growth; but on poor sites, better growth at wide spacings versus close spacings may be common.

The response of ponderosa pine to various densities is complicated by interacting factors—response to thinning, differences in initial tree size, interactions between tree size and density levels, competing tree sizes, shrub competition, site productivity, and the selection effect. Studies that consider many factors together are insightful. Uzoh and Oliver (2006) analyzed data from long-term permanent research plots in even-aged, pure stands of planted and natural ponderosa pine. There were six levels of density in stands throughout the species range in the western United States. Ponderosa pine height increment decreased with increasing Stand Density Index (SDI, a measure of density), but SDI was the least important of the seven variables in the equation. Other variables predicting height growth were site index, dbh, dbh^2, the interaction of slope and aspect, elevation, and basal area in larger trees (BAL). Because the equation included BAL, which is a measure of the tree's position relative to other trees in a plot or stand, Uzoh and Oliver felt that SDI represents the effect of density on height growth of all trees in the stand regardless of tree size.

Thus, while there is no consensus on the effect of spacing on ponderosa pine height growth, it is clear from the literature that the effect of spacing on height growth is not as pronounced as the effect of spacing on diameter growth. Our finding of no spacing effect on height growth likely results from choosing sample trees that were leave trees in operationally thinned-from-below stands or, in the case of the controls, that would have been leave trees.

Height/diameter ratios

An H/D ratio is the quotient quantifying a unit of height per unit of diameter. These ratios have been used to determine when trees are susceptible to snow and wind damage. For example, Wonn and O'Hara (2001) found that four northern Rocky Mountain conifer species (including ponderosa pine) were more prone to stem bending and breakage when H/D ratios were 80:1 (ft:ft) or higher. Slender trees develop in higher stand densities; thus, H/D ratios can be controlled silviculturally by managing stand density. Increased stand density results in height growth at the expense of diameter growth as trees try to attain or retain apical dominance (Henry and Aarssen 1999; Wonn and O'Hara 2001). Evidence has accumulated that trees "perceive" competition from neighboring plants through the phytochrome system (e.g., Ritchie 1997; Henry and Aarssen 1999). The light reflected from competitor foliage has a reduced red:far red ratio compared to solar radiation, which provides trees with a signal of nearby competition even before shading occurs.

Because H/D ratios are a function of density, they can be used to study response to thinning and as an indicator of competition. Our data show that H/D ratios increased in the 5 yrs after thinning in the control plots (Table 6), indicating that trees may be responding to inter-tree competition. Average H/D ratios remained statistically unchanged in the 5x5 and 7x7 spacings but decreased significantly in the 10x10 and 14x14 spacings. To obtain a significant decrease in H/D ratios, thinning to at least 10x10 spacing is appropriate for ponderosa pine seedlings and saplings on these types of sites.

H_{grow}/D_{grow} ratios decreased rapidly with increasing spacing (Table 7), from 101.5 in the control to 38.2 in the 14x14. The ratio declined from 101.5 to 93.8 between the control and 5x5, followed by a decline of 31.5 from the 5x5 to the 7x7 spacing. Between the 7x7 and 10x10 spacings, the average ratio declined by 10.3, followed by a decline of 13.8 between the 10x10 and 14x14 spacings. Because we found that spacing affected dbh growth but not height growth, we conclude that at least a 7x7 spacing is necessary to stimulate significant diameter growth response in these types of sites.

Reukema and Smith (1987) found that height/diameter ratios were influenced by spacing in plantations in British Columbia. Douglas-fir, western redcedar, and western hemlock had higher ratios (slender trees) at closer spacings, which agree with our results for ponderosa pine.

Change in crown ratios

The two variables important in predicting 5-yr change in crown ratio (CR_Δ) are beginning crown ratio (CR_{HCB}) and density. Density can be expressed as either spacing or residual basal area (BA_t). Wider spacings or lower basal area result in lengthening crown ratios.

Reukema and Smith (1987) found in plantation spacing trials that wider spacings resulted in higher crown ratios for Douglas-fir and western redcedar. However, spacing had no effect on crown ratios for western hemlock.

Crown ratios are a morphological indicator of individual tree vigor and have been used to predict tree growth (e.g., Wykoff 1986; Ferguson 1988; Wykoff 1990). In forest growth models (Wykoff and others 1982; Crookston and Dixon 2005), crown ratio can be used to differentiate tree growth through successive time periods.

Height to crown base

Height to crown base (HCB) has become increasingly important for rating stand risk to wildfire and prescribed fire, for predicting wood quality, and for including in forest growth models such as the Fire and Fuels Extension to the Forest Vegetation Simulator (FFE-FVS, Reinhardt and Crookston 2003). To date, information is generally lacking for this tree attribute and how it changes through management. Fortunately, HCB can be calculated if tree height and crown ratio are known.

HCB changes with post-thin density, beginning tree crown ratio (CR_0), and initial tree diameter (D_0). Trees within spacings tended to respond similarly. HCB increased more at higher densities than at lower densities, showing that the distance between the ground and the base of crowns can be silviculturally managed through density control. Also, HCB values had less variation at wider spacings than at narrower spacings, showing that trees in narrower spacings were differentiating more so than those in wider spacings. Tradeoffs exist between having high-density stands with high crown bases versus low-density stands with low crown bases because high crowns decrease fire hazard to trees, but high density increases fire hazard. Conceivably, dense stands could be thinned enough to lower H/D ratios, and then thinned again when crown bases reach a pre-determined height.

The cumulative percentage distributions of HCB_5 shown in Figure 6 may be helpful in assessing the tradeoffs between HCB and density. For example, the cumulative distributions for the control (Figure 6a) show that about 30% of the trees had an HCB greater than 5 ft at the time of thinning. Five yrs later, about 75% of the trees had an HCB greater than 5 ft. Therefore, if an HCB of 5 ft or more was the target, an additional 45% of the trees attained this value after 5 yrs.

Hann and Hanus (2004) developed HCB_Δ equations for untreated Douglas-fir stands in southwestern British Columbia, western Washington, and northwestern Oregon. Crown ratio and stand density were also important in their equations, as well as stand age. In a study of thinned loblolly pine (*Pinus taeda*) in Virginia, Peterson and others (1997) found that lower branches remained alive longer in thinned stands. While live crowns in control stands decreased 30%, crown ratios in thinned stands decreased only 14%. The slower rate of decrease in the thinned stands was attributed to survival of lower branches. Crown recession occurs when branches at the base of the crown are shaded by competitors, which is primarily a function of density. Garber and others (2008) developed crown recession models for three conifer species in northern Idaho, including ponderosa pine. Crown ratio was the most important predictor of HCB_Δ, with crown recession increasing with greater crown ratios, which agrees with our study results.

Shoot borer damage

About one-quarter of the trees had shoot borer damage within the 5-yr period after thinning. Site elevation was the best predictor of shoot borer damage, with lower elevations correlated with an increasing probability of shoot borer occurrence. While we had only seven sites, and therefore seven elevations, we left elevation in the equation because of its known importance for predicting shoot borer damage. Other authors (Stoszek 1973; Robertson and Dewey 1983) have noted that dry, lower-elevation sites have a higher incidence of shoot borer damage than more mesic, higher-elevation sites. Within the range of elevations and site conditions in this study, we feel the use of elevation in Eq. 5 should work well.

Shoot borer damage is positively correlated with tree characteristics ($H\text{-}5_{grow}$ and CR_0) and negatively correlated with post-thin treatment basal area (BA_t). In northern Idaho and western Montana, Robertson and Dewey (1983) also found that trees with better height growth rates had higher infestation levels; however, unlike our results, they found a negative correlation between infestation rate and height growth. Sower and Shorb (1984) explained that shoot borer infestation may appear to have no effect on height growth because larger trees or larger terminal buds are more likely to be selected by females as oviposition sites. Potential elongation of the terminal on larger trees or buds is greater than on smaller trees or buds, but actual elongation is decreased by bud mining. Therefore, direct comparison of infested and uninfested shoots may show no difference in growth.

Even though we found statistical significance for the prediction of shoot borer damage and the equation makes biological sense, trees that had shoot borer damage often appeared no different than undamaged trees. Perhaps factors other than tree and site characteristics were controlling shoot borer dispersion, survival, and colonization success.

Growth anomaly and climate

An anomaly became apparent when examining height growth data. As shown in Table 3, average 5-yr pre-thin height growth (H-5$_{grow}$) was 6.9 ft, while average 5-yr post-thin height growth (H$_{grow}$) was 5.0 ft. This is counter-intuitive because the thinning-from-below should have made more resources available for tree growth. A further breakdown of the data showed that average height growth at the Nez Perce sites was 5.8 ft before thinning and 5.4 ft after thinning. Average height growth at the Spokane sites was 8.2 ft before thinning and 4.5 ft after thinning.

We examined the data for possible explanations for the growth decline. The decline was across all spacings, including the control, so it was not a response to thinning. Also, the decline was not related to shoot borer damage.

We were able to examine site climate patterns using techniques of Rehfeldt (2006) and Rehfeldt and others (2009). Data from western weather stations were used to develop thin plate spline surfaces to estimate monthly climate variables for the seven study sites. The monthly predictions were then averaged to produce yearly temperature and precipitation estimates, as well as growing season precipitation and temperature. Eighteen variables were predicted, as defined by Rehfeldt (2006).

Analyses of the climate data showed that the Spokane sites had an elevated growing season dryness index (GSDI) following thinning, while the Nez Perce sites did not (Figure 8). GSDI is calculated as the square root of growing season degree days that are greater than 5 °C divided by growing season precipitation. It has been used to predict conifer occurrence and abundance in the Inland Northwest (Rehfeldt and others 2008). Higher GSDI values indicate drier conditions during the growing season. Average GSDI for the 5-yr pre-thin period at the three Spokane sites was 0.263, and it was 0.386 for the 5-yr post-thin period. Average GSDI for the 5-yr pre-thin period at the four Nez Perce sites was 0.108, and it was 0.135 for the 5-yr post-thin period.

Because annual shoot growth is determined by the number of needle primordia formed in the bud in the previous year, moisture stress during the growing season could result in poor terminal bud formation, which translates into less shoot elongation the following growing season (Lanner 1985). Therefore, high GSDI values at the Spokane sites could account for the slower-than-expected height growth. We feel that slower height growth after thinning at the Spokane sites did not affect our conclusions.

Non-Tree Vegetation and Thinning Slash

The forbs, grasses, and shrubs recorded during the course of this study are typical for these types of sites. There were no dramatic vegetation responses to the thinnings between yrs 1 and 5, with a few exceptions. For example, epilobium and vetch had steady increments in occurrence from the control to larger increases at wider spacings, and strawberry had a substantial decrease in the control with no corresponding decrease in the thinned areas (Table 13). Coast tarweed and dandelion had large increases across all spacings.

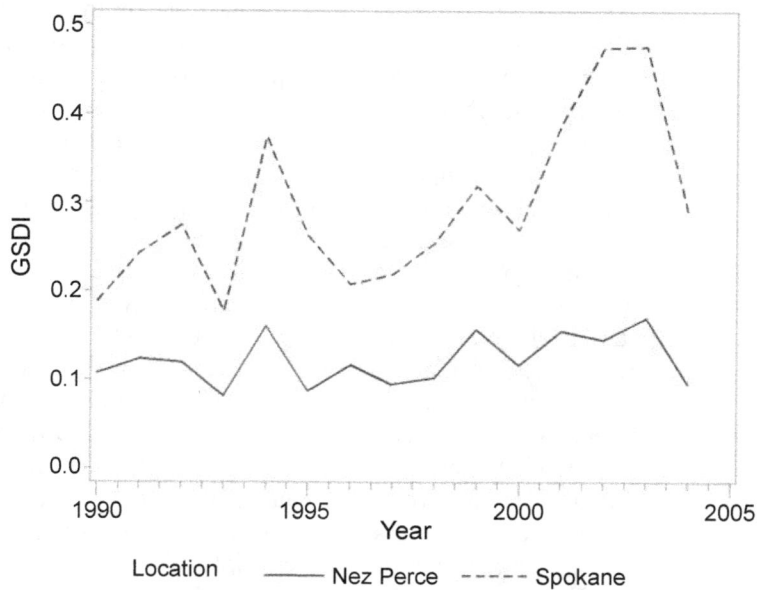

Figure 8. Average growing season dryness index (GSDI) by year for the Nez Perce and Spokane study sites.

The invasive species spotted knapweed actually decreased across spacings, but this may have been due to the apparently successful introduction of two biological control insects that were released in 2001 and 2002 near the two Castle Rock sites.

Our separate analyses of shrub occurrence, cover, and height helped determine if species were becoming established on additional plots, increasing in coverage, and/or growing in height. Only serviceberry had consistently large increases in occurrence in thinned areas; however, there was also a large increase in the control, suggesting favorable conditions during the time period of this study (Table 14).

Although generally positive, no shrub species had increases in coverage greater than 5%, and increased coverage in the controls was often as good as, or better than, in the thinned areas (Table 14). Shrub species did not respond much in percent cover between yrs 1 and 5 after thinning.

Shrub heights generally increased between yr 1 and yr 5, but again not significantly (Table 14). Serviceberry grew 0.81, 0.72, and 1.04 ft at the three wider spacings; black hawthorn had the best height growth in the control; and roses increased between 0.16 and 0.51 ft in height at all spacings. Snowberry was, by far, the most dominant shrub species on these sites, but the response to thinning was nil (Table 14).

Griffis and others (2001) found little difference in understory vegetation between unthinned and thinned stands in Arizona. Unlike our young stands, their stands were mature, even-aged ponderosa pine. Their thinned stands averaged 81 ft^2 basal area/acre and 772 stems/acre, while the unthinned stands averaged 139 ft^2 basal area/acre and 1968 stems/acre. The authors speculated that the thinnings, which removed at least 30% of the basal area, may not have reduced density enough to result in a response in the understory.

Vegetation responses to thinning are confounded by a number of factors, including variation in weather from year to year, herbivory, secondary succession, and site productivity. For example, we noted that small black hawthorn plants were repeatedly browsed to groundline. Whatever response black hawthorn may have had to thinning was masked by intense preferential browsing of this species. Other species may be similarly limited in their ability to respond to thinnings. Animal exclosures would be useful to assess the effect of herbivory on vegetation response following thinning.

Although we did not control competing vegetation in this study, other researchers have noted an important tradeoff that may influence the timing and amount of thinning. In a northern California study of thinning 11-yr-old ponderosa pine, Oliver (1984) found no trend of increasing shrub growth as stand density decreased, which agrees with our results. However, he found that increasing shrub density restricted tree diameter and height growth. Above a threshold value of about 30% cover, shrub competition negated any positive effects of spacing on tree growth. The tradeoff is that stem quality and form factors can be improved at wider spacings with shrub competition (Oliver 1990). Ponderosa pine branch diameters in plots with shrubs averaged 71% of branch diameters in plots without shrubs. Busse and others (1996) found that understory vegetation negatively affected growth of ponderosa pine for the first 20 yrs after thinning to release suppressed ponderosa pine saplings in central Oregon. The authors also noted a long-term benefit to the upper soil horizon associated with maintaining understory vegetation versus long-term vegetation removal.

We feel that the generally mild responses of vegetation to thinning in this study are typical for sites where trees are felled with chainsaws. Ground disturbance in this study was minimal, which reduced potential sites for establishment of competing and invasive species. Other types of thinning, such as the use of heavy equipment or fire, would increase the amount of soil disturbance and, therefore, the potential for establishment of vegetation. Still, it was somewhat surprising that already established shrubs did not expand more in response to the thinning. Perhaps ungulate browsing prevented shrub response in these relatively small treatment units, whereas larger treatment units may have resulted in browsing being spread across larger areas. Perhaps the size of shrub plants was already near maximum at the time of thinning, so little response could be expected. Oliver's (1984) finding that shrub growth did not decrease with increasing stand density may provide an explanation. He felt that perhaps shrubs were better at exploiting site resources than ponderosa pine saplings in northern California, thus the trees had little effect on the shrubs.

Ponderosa pine thinning slash had higher occurrences along line transects at wider spacings (Table 13). This was expected because more trees were cut and left on sites at wider spacings (except for a few plots at West Talmaks, where the slash was removed to eliminate problems with pine engraver beetles). Occurrences varied from 81% in the 5x5 spacing to 94% in the 14x14 spacing. Percent cover increased at wider spacings (9% in the 5x5 to 17% in the 10x10; Table 15). Percent cover dropped rapidly by yr 3 as the needles and fine twigs decomposed following thinning, then remained constant through yr 5 (Figure 7). An increase in fine fuels following thinning, which decay and are quickly incorporated into forest litter, was expected and has been documented by others (Youngblood and others 2008).

Conclusions

These are naturally regenerated, operationally thinned ponderosa pine stands on relatively dry sites. Seedling- and sapling-size trees were thinned from below to leave the largest and most vigorous trees as evenly spaced as possible. Managers should expect similar results when pre-commercially thinning stands like those in this study.

Prior to thinning, these stands were very dense (2469 to 10,128 trees/acre). Trees were maintaining height growth at the expense of diameter growth, resulting in high H/D ratios (slender trees) and small crown ratios. After thinning, a few trees (1.6%)

with high H/D ratios developed severe lean. Only 3% of the trees died during the 5-yr period after thinning; these trees had high H/D ratios, small pre-thin height growth, and small crown ratios.

Fortunately, there are pre-thin morphological indicators of tree vigor that can be used to predict post-thin response. Larger trees and trees with larger crown ratios at the time of thinning are associated with larger post-thin diameter and height growth. Larger pre-thin height growth is associated with larger post-thin height growth.

Lowering the density of stands by thinning results in important changes in tree growth. Wider spacings were associated with larger diameter growth, which resulted in lower H/D ratios because spacing did not influence height growth. Wider spacings were also associated with larger crown ratios and crown bases closer to the ground because lower branches did not die as rapidly at wide spacings as they did at narrow spacings. At least a 10x10 ft spacing was required to obtain a significant lowering of H/D ratios during the 5-yr period.

Western pine shoot borer damage was recorded on one-quarter of the trees, but there was no statistical difference in height or diameter growth between infested and uninfested trees. Increased shoot borer damage was associated with larger crown ratios and larger pre-thin height growth. Damage was higher at lower densities and lower elevations.

Other vegetation growing in association with these ponderosa pine trees did not markedly change in response to the thinnings. Also, there was not an increase in non-native invasive plant species. The lack of shrub, grass, and forb response was perhaps due to a combination of herbivory and the lack of ground disturbance during the thinning operations.

References

Avery, T. E.; Burkhart, H. E. 1983. Forest Measurements, Third Edition. New York, NY: McGraw-Hill, Inc. 331 p.

Barrett, J. W. 1982. Twenty-year growth of ponderosa pine saplings thinned to five spacings in central Oregon. Res. Pap. PNW-301. Portland, OR: USDA Forest Service, Pacific Northwest Forest and Range Experiment Station. 18 p.

Baskerville, G. L. 1972. Use of logarithmic regression in the estimation of plant biomass. Canadian Journal of Forest Research. 2:49-53.

Busse, M. D.; Cochran, P. H.; Barrett, J. W. 1996. Changes in ponderosa pine site productivity following removal of understory vegetation. Soil Science Society of America Journal. 60:1614-1621.

Canfield, R. H. 1941. Application of the line interception method in sampling range vegetation. Journal of Forestry. 39:388-394.

Chambers, J. C.; Brown, R. W. 1983. Methods for vegetation sampling and analysis on revegetated mined lands. Gen. Tech. Rep. INT-151. Ogden, UT: USDA Forest Service, Intermountain Forest and Range Experiment Station. 57 p.

Cochran, P. H.; Barrett, J. W. 1999. Growth of ponderosa pine thinned to different stocking levels in central Oregon: 30-year results. Res. Pap. PNW-508. Portland, OR: USDA Forest Service, Pacific Northwest Research Station. 27 p.

Cooper, S. V.; Neiman, K. E.; Roberts, D. W. 1991. Forest habitat types of northern Idaho: a second approximation. Gen. Tech. Rep. INT-236. Ogden, UT: USDA Forest Service, Intermountain Research Station. 143 p.

Crookston, N. L.; Dixon, G. E. 2005. The Forest Vegetation Simulator: a review of its structure, content, and applications. Computers and Electronics in Agriculture. 49:60-80.

Daubenmire, R. 1959. A canopy-coverage method of vegetation analysis. Northwest Science. 33:43-64.

Ferguson, D. E. 1988. Growth of regeneration defoliated by spruce budworm in Idaho. Res. Pap. INT-393. Ogden, UT: USDA Forest Service, Intermountain Research Station. 13 p.

Garber, S. M.; Monserud, R. A.; Maguire, D. A. 2008. Crown recession patterns in three conifer species of the northern Rocky Mountains. Forest Science. 54:633-646.

Griffis, K. L.; Crawford, J. A.; Wagner, M. R.; Moir, W. H. 2001. Understory response to management treatments in northern Arizona ponderosa pine forests. Forest Ecology and Management. 146:239-245.

Hann, D. W.; Hanus, M. L. 2004. Evaluation of nonspatial approaches and equation forms used to predict tree crown recession. Canadian Journal of Forest Research 34:1993-2003.

Harrington, T. B.; Harrington, C. A.; DeBell, D. S. 2009. Effects of planting spacing and site quality on 25-year growth and mortality relationships of Douglas-fir (*Pseudotsuga menziesii* var. *menziesii*). Forest Ecology and Management. 258:18-25.

Henry, H. A. L.; Aarssen, L. W. 1999. The interpretation of stem diameter-height allometry in trees: biomechanical constraints, neighbour effects, or biased regressions? Ecology Letters. 2:89-97.

Hynynen, J. 1995. Predicting the growth response to thinning for Scots pine stands using individual-tree growth models. Silva Fennica. 29:225-246.

Johnson, F.A. 1956. Use of a bark thickness–tree diameter relationship for estimating past diameters of ponderosa pine trees. Res. Note PNW-126. Portland, OR: USDA Forest Service, Pacific Northwest Forest and Range Experiment Station. 3 p.

Johnstone, W. D. 1981. Effects of spacing 7-year old lodgepole pine in west-central Alberta. Info. Rep. NOR-X-236. Edmonton, Alberta, Canada: Northern Forest Research Centre. 18 p.

Kirk, R. E. 1982. Experimental Design, Second Edition. Brook/Cole Publishing Company, Monterey, CA. 911 p.

Lanner, R. M. 1985. On the insensitivity of height growth to spacing. Forest Ecology and Management. 13:143-148.

Littell, R. C.; Milliken, G. A.; Stroup, W. W.; Wolfinger, R. D. 1996. SAS system for mixed models. SAS Institute, Cary, NC. 633 p.

Livingston, R. L. 1979. The pine engraver in Idaho. Life history, habits and management recommendations. Report 79-3. Coeur d'Alene, ID: Idaho Department of Lands, Forest and Insect Control. 7 p.

Meyer, W. H. 1934. Growth in selectively cut ponderosa pine forests of the Pacific Northwest. Tech. Bull. 407. Washington, DC: USDA Forest Service. 64 p.

Oliver, C. D.; Larson, B. C. 1990. Forest Stand Dynamics. New York, NY: McGraw-Hill, Inc. 467 p.

Oliver, W. W. 1979. Growth of planted ponderosa pine thinned to different stocking levels in northern California. Res. Pap. PSW-147. Berkeley, CA: USDA Forest Service, Pacific Southwest Forest and Range Experiment Station. 11 p.

Oliver, W. W. 1984. Brush reduces growth of thinned ponderosa pine in northern California. Res. Pap. PSW-172. Berkeley, CA: USDA Forest Service, Pacific Southwest Forest and Range Experiment Station. 7 p.

Oliver, W. W. 1990. Spacing and shrub competition influence 20-year development of planted ponderosa pine. Western Journal of Applied Forestry. 5:79-82.

Oliver, W. W. 1997. Twenty-five-year growth and mortality of planted ponderosa pine repeatedly thinned to different stand densities in northern California. Western Journal of Applied Forestry. 12:122-130.

Oliver, W. W.; Ryker, R. A. 1990. *Pinus ponderosa* Dougl. ex Laws. In: Burns, R. M.; Honkala, B. H., tech. coords. Silvics of North America: 1. Conifers. Agric. Handb. 654. Washington, DC: USDA Forest Service: 413-424.

Peterson, J. A.; Seiler, J. R.; Nowak, J.; Ginn, S. E.; Kreh, R. E. 1997. Growth and physiological responses of young loblolly pine stands to thinning. Forest Science. 43:529-534

Pfister, R. D.; Kovalchik, B. L.; Arno, S. F.; Presby, R. C. 1977. Forest habitat types of Montana. Gen. Tech. Rep. INT-34. Ogden, UT: USDA Forest Service, Intermountain Forest and Range Experiment Station. 174 p.

Rehfeldt, G. E. 1991. A model of genetic variation for *Pinus ponderosa* in the Inland Northwest (U.S.A.): applications in gene resource management. Canadian Journal of Forest Research. 21:1491-1500.

Rehfeldt, G. E. 2006. A spline model of climate for the western United States. Gen. Tech. Rep. RMRS-165. Fort Collins, CO: USDA Forest Service, Rocky Mountain Research Station. 21 p.

Rehfeldt, G. E.; Ferguson, D. E.; Crookston, N. L. 2008. Quantifying the abundance of co-occurring conifers along Inland Northwest (USA) climate gradients. Ecology. 89:2127-2139.

Rehfeldt, G. E.; Ferguson, D. E.; Crookston, N. L. 2009. Aspen, climate, and sudden decline in western USA. Forest Ecology and Management. 258:2353-2364.

Reinhardt, E.; Crookston, N. L., tech. eds. 2003. The Fire and Fuels Extension to the Forest Vegetation Simulator. Gen. Tech. Rep. RMRS-116. Ogden, UT: USDA Forest Service, Rocky Mountain Research Station. 209 p.

Reukema, D. L. 1979. Fifty-year development of Douglas-fir stands planted at various spacings. Res. Pap. PNW-253. Portland, OR: USDA Forest Service, Pacific Northwest Forest and Range Experiment Station. 21 p.

Reukema, D. L.; Smith, J. H. G. 1987. Development over 25 years of Douglas-fir, western hemlock, and western redcedar planted at various spacings on a very good site in British Columbia. Res. Pap. PNW-381. Portland, OR: USDA Forest Service, Pacific Northwest Research Station. 46 p.

Ritchie, G. A. 1997. Evidence for red:far red signaling and photomorphogenic growth response in Douglas-fir (*Pseudotsuga menziesii*) seedlings. Tree Physiology. 17:161-168.

Robertson, A. S.; Dewey, J. E. 1983. Determination of western shoot borer incidence, impact, and stand hazard rating characteristics in selected Region One National Forests. Report 83-10. Missoula, MT: USDA Forest Service, Northern Region, State and Private Forestry. 13 p.

Ronco, F., Jr.; Edminster, C. B.; Trujillo, D. P. 1985. Growth of ponderosa pine thinned to different stocking levels in northern Arizona. Res. Pap. RM-262. Fort Collins, CO: USDA Forest Service, Rocky Mountain Forest and Range Experiment Station. 15 p.

Scott, J. H.; Reinhardt, E. D. 2001. Assessing crown fire potential by linking models of surface and crown fire behavior. Res. Pap. RMRS-RP-29. Fort Collins, CO: USDA Forest Service, Rocky Mountain Research Station. 59 p.

Sower, L. L.; Shorb, M. D. 1984. Effect of western pine shoot borer (Lepidoptera: Olethreutidae) on vertical growth of ponderosa pine. Journal of Economic Entomology. 77:932-935.

Stoszek, K. J. 1973. Damage to ponderosa pine plantations by the western pine shoot borer. Journal of Forestry. 71:701-705.

Uzoh, F. C. C.; Oliver, W. W. 2006. Individual tree height increment model for managed even-aged stands of ponderosa pine throughout the western United States using linear mixed effects models. Forest Ecology and Management. 221:147-154.

Van Deusen, J. L. 1968. Periodic growth of pole-sized ponderosa pine as related to thinning and selected environmental factors. Res. Pap. RM-38. Fort Collins, CO: USDA Forest Service, Rocky Mountain Forest and Range Experiment Station. 12 p.

Wagner, R. G.; Radosevich, S. R. 1991. Interspecific competition and other factors influencing the performance of Douglas-fir saplings in the Oregon Coast Range. Canadian Journal of Forestry Research. 21:829-835.

Williams, C. K.; Kelley, B. F.; Smith, B. G.; Lillybridge, T. R. 1995. Forested plant associations of the Colville National Forest. Gen. Tech. Rep. PNW-360. Portland, OR: USDA Forest Service, Pacific Northwest Research Station. 375 p.

Wonn, H. T.; O'Hara, K. L. 2001. Height:diameter ratios and stability relationships for four northern Rocky Mountain tree species. Western Journal of Applied Forestry. 16:87-94.

Wykoff, W. R. 1986. Supplement to the user's guide for the Stand Prognosis Model–version 5.0. Gen. Tech. Rep. INT-208. Ogden, UT: USDA Forest Service, Intermountain Research Station. 36 p.

Wykoff, W. R. 1990. A basal area increment model for individual conifers in the northern Rocky Mountains. Forest Science. 36:1077-1104.

Wykoff, W. R.; Crookston, N. L.; Stage, A. R. 1982. User's guide to the Stand Prognosis Model. Gen. Tech. Rep. INT-133. Ogden, UT: USDA Forest Service, Intermountain Forest and Range Experiment Station. 112 p.

Youngblood, A.; Wright, C. S.; Ottmar, R. D.; McIver, J. D. 2008. Changes in fuelbed characteristics and resulting fire potentials after fuel reduction treatments in dry forests of the Blue Mountains, northeastern Oregon. Forest Ecology and Management. 255:3151-3169.

www.ingramcontent.com/pod-product-compliance
Lightning Source LLC
Chambersburg PA
CBHW081135280526
45787CB00007B/3096

* 9 781507 666364 *